MULTICULTURA

JAMES A. BA

From Foster Care to College: Navigating Educational Challenges and Creating Possibilities
ROYEL M. JOHNSON

Achieving Equal Educational Opportunity for Students of Color: Disrupting Structural Racism—An American Imperative
RICHARD R. VALENCIA

Critical Multicultural Education: Theory and Practice
CHRISTINE E. SLEETER

Race and Media Literacy, Explained (or Why Does the Black Guy Die First?)
FREDERICK W. GOODING, JR.

Whiteness in the Ivory Tower: Why *Don't* We Notice the White Students Sitting Together in the Quad?
NOLAN L. CABRERA

Culturally Sustaining Policymaking in Indigenous Communities: Partnering to Promote Lasting Change
APRILLE J. PHILLIPS

Educating for Equity and Excellence: Enacting Culturally Responsive Teaching
GENEVA GAY

Speculative Pedagogies: Designing Equitable Educational Futures
ANTERO GARCIA & NICOLE MIRRA, EDS.

Seeing Whiteness: The Essential Essays of Robin DiAngelo
ROBIN DIANGELO

Becoming an Antiracist School Leader: Dare to Be Real
PATRICK A. DUFFY

The Hip-Hop Mindset: Success Strategies for Educators and Other Professionals
TOBY S. JENKINS

Education for Liberal Democracy: Using Classroom Discussion to Build Knowledge and Voice
WALTER C. PARKER

Critical Race Theory and Its Critics: Implications for Research and Teaching
FRANCESCA LÓPEZ & CHRISTINE E. SLEETER

Anti-Blackness at School: Creating Affirming Educational Spaces for African American Students
JOI A. SPENCER & KERRI ULLUCCI

Sustaining Disabled Youth: Centering Disability in Asset Pedagogies
FEDERICO R. WAITOLLER & KATHLEEN A. KING THORIUS, EDS.

The Civil Rights Road to Deeper Learning: Five Essentials for Equity
KIA DARLING-HAMMOND & LINDA DARLING-HAMMOND

Reckoning With Racism in Family–School Partnerships: Centering Black Parents' School Engagement
JENNIFER L. MCCARTHY FOUBERT

Teaching Anti-Fascism: A Critical Multicultural Pedagogy for Civic Engagement
MICHAEL VAVRUS

Unsettling Settler-Colonial Education: The Transformational Indigenous Praxis Model
CORNEL PEWEWARDY, ANNA LEES, & ROBIN ZAPE-TAH-HOL-AH MINTHORN, EDS.

Culturally and Socially Responsible Assessment: Theory, Research, and Practice
CATHERINE S. TAYLOR, WITH SUSAN B. NOLEN

LGBTQ Youth and Education: Policies and Practices, 2nd Ed.
CRIS MAYO

Transforming Multicultural Education Policy and Practice: Expanding Educational Opportunity
JAMES A. BANKS, ED.

Critical Race Theory in Education: A Scholar's Journey
GLORIA LADSON-BILLINGS

Civic Education in the Age of Mass Migration: Implications for Theory and Practice
ANGELA M. BANKS

Creating a Home in Schools: Sustaining Identities for Black, Indigenous, and Teachers of Color
FRANCISCO RIOS & A LONGORIA

Generation Mixed Goes to School: Radically Listening to Multiracial Kids
RALINA L. JOSEPH & ALLISON BRISCOE-SMITH

Race, Culture, and Politics in Education: A Global Journey from South Africa
KOGILA MOODLEY

Indian Education for All: Decolonizing Indigenous Education in Public Schools
JOHN P. HOPKINS

Racial Microaggressions: Using Critical Race Theory to Respond to Everyday Racism
DANIEL G. SOLÓRZANO & LINDSAY PÉREZ HUBER

City Schools and the American Dream 2: The Enduring Promise of Public Education
PEDRO A. NOGUERA & ESA SYEED

For a complete list of series titles, please visit www.tcpress.com/MCE

(continued)

Multicultural Education Series, *continued*

Measuring Race
Robert T. Teranishi et al.

Campus Uprisings
Ty-Ron M. O. Douglas et al.

Transformative Ethnic Studies in Schools
Christine E. Sleeter & Miguel Zavala

Why Race and Culture Matter in Schools, 2nd Ed.
Tyrone C. Howard

Just Schools
Ann M. Ishimaru

Immigrant-Origin Students in Community College
Carola Suárez-Orozco & Olivia Osei-Twumasi, Eds.

"We Dare Say Love"
Na'ilah Suad Nasir et al., Eds.

Teaching What *Really* Happened, 2nd Ed.
James W. Loewen

Culturally Responsive Teaching, 3rd Ed.
Geneva Gay

Music, Education, and Diversity
Patricia Shehan Campbell

Reaching and Teaching Students in Poverty, 2nd Ed.
Paul C. Gorski

Deconstructing Race
Jabari Mahiri

Is Everyone Really Equal? 2nd Ed.
Özlem Sensoy & Robin DiAngelo

Transforming Educational Pathways for Chicana/o Students
Dolores Delgado Bernal & Enrique Alemán Jr.

Un-Standardizing Curriculum, 2nd Ed.
Christine E. Sleeter & Judith Flores Carmona

Global Migration, Diversity, and Civic Education
James A. Banks et al., Eds.

Reclaiming the Multicultural Roots of U.S. Curriculum
Wayne Au et al.

Human Rights and Schooling
Audrey Osler

We Can't Teach What We Don't Know, 3rd Ed.
Gary R. Howard

Diversity and Education
Michael Vavrus

Mathematics for Equity
Na'ilah Suad Nasir et al., Eds.

Race, Empire, and English Language Teaching
Suhanthie Motha

Black Male(d)
Tyrone C. Howard

Race Frameworks
Zeus Leonardo

Class Rules
Peter W. Cookson Jr.

Streetsmart Schoolsmart
Gilberto Q. Conchas & James Diego Vigil

Achieving Equity for Latino Students
Frances Contreras

Literacy Achievement and Diversity
Kathryn H. Au

Understanding English Language Variation in U.S. Schools
Anne H. Charity Hudley & Christine Mallinson

Latino Children Learning English
Guadalupe Valdés et al.

Asians in the Ivory Tower
Robert T. Teranishi

Diversity and Equity in Science Education
Okhee Lee & Cory A. Buxton

Forbidden Language
Patricia Gándara & Megan Hopkins, Eds.

The Light in Their Eyes, 10th Anniversary Ed.
Sonia Nieto

The Flat World and Education
Linda Darling-Hammond

Educating Citizens in a Multicultural Society, 2nd Ed.
James A. Banks

Culture, Literacy, and Learning
Carol D. Lee

Facing Accountability in Education
Christine E. Sleeter, Ed.

Talkin Black Talk
H. Samy Alim & John Baugh, Eds.

Improving Access to Mathematics
Na'ilah Suad Nasir & Paul Cobb, Eds.

"To Remain an Indian"
K. Tsianina Lomawaima & Teresa L. McCarty

Beyond the Big House
Gloria Ladson-Billings

Teaching and Learning in Two Languages
Eugene E. García

Improving Multicultural Education
Cherry A. McGee Banks

Transforming the Multicultural Education of Teachers
Michael Vavrus

Learning to Teach for Social Justice
Linda Darling-Hammond et al., Eds.

Learning and Not Learning English
Guadalupe Valdés

The Children Are Watching
Carlos E. Cortés

Multicultural Education, Transformative Knowledge, and Action
James A. Banks, Ed.

From Foster Care to College

Navigating Educational Challenges and Creating Possibilities

Royel M. Johnson

Series Foreword by James A. Banks

Published by Teachers College Press,® 1234 Amsterdam Avenue,
New York, NY 10027

Front cover photos: Student by 4x6 / iStock by Getty Images; college by Kevin Dooley / Flickr Creative Commons; backpack by Davyd Bortnik / Pexels.

Library of Congress Cataloging-in-Publication Data

Names: Johnson, Royel M., author.
Title: From foster care to college : navigating educational challenges and creating possibilities / Royel M. Johnson ; series foreword by James A. Banks.
Description: New York : Teachers College Press, [2024] | Series: Multicultural education series | Includes bibliographical references and index.
Identifiers: LCCN 2024027013 (print) | LCCN 2024027014 (ebook) | ISBN 9780807786062 (paper ; acid-free paper) | ISBN 9780807786079 (hardcover ; acid-free paper) | ISBN 9780807782576 (epub)
Subjects: LCSH: Foster children—Education (Higher)—United States—Case studies.
Classification: LCC LC4091 .J625 2024 (print) | LCC LC4091 (ebook) | DDC 378.1/98092554—dc23/eng/20240715
LC record available at https://lccn.loc.gov/2024027013
LC ebook record available at https://lccn.loc.gov/2024027014

ISBN 978-0-8077-8606-2 (paper)
ISBN 978-0-8077-8607-9 (hardcover)
ISBN 978-0-8077-8257-6 (ebook)

Printed on acid-free paper
Manufactured in the United States of America

In loving memory of my late aunt, Pricilla Ann Echols, the very first writer and author who ignited my passion for storytelling when I was child. I made a promise to you that I would bring this book to life. This is for you, Aunt "Ann."

Contents

Foreword

In a society that purports to value its young, the United States has a disturbing approach to supporting some of its most vulnerable youth. Youth in foster care are one of the groups that immediately come to mind. There are little under 400,000 young people in foster care in this country, and many of the accounts provided by people in this system are not always positive.

The history of the foster care system in the United States is deeply layered and complex, and dates back to the 19th century. While often thought of as a benevolent system that provides care, shelter, and sustenance for parentless children, or a system that removes children from physically abusive parents, there is a more nuanced reality that is vital to understanding foster care and young people's experience of it.

To be fair, there have been countless people who have benefited from positive experiences in the system and have received ongoing love, care, and support from dedicated, nurturing, and selfless adults. However, a more complete narrative must consider the history of a system that has been replete with obstacles, bureaucracies, systemic exclusion, and histories of racism for many young people and their families.

Dating back to slavery, there has been an intentional and persistent effort of tearing apart Black families in particular. In the United States, Black children were often viewed as property with high value that contributed to the institution of slavery. Thus, removing Black children from homes has a dark and ugly history in the United States, and in many instances the current system of foster care has some similarities (Roberts, 2001).

So, what does that mean for today's foster care system? Some would say it is a system that does more harm than good. Others have hesitated to refer to it as a system of "care" when it often unnecessarily removes children from their families, and instead see it as a system that inflicts intentional harm on many Black and Indigenous youth (Harvey, 2023). Legal scholar Dorothy Roberts (2022) refers to the foster care system as a family policing system that inflicts indelible harm on Black children and families; she has been persistent in her call for abolishing this system. Roberts is not alone; education scholars Brianna Harvey and Kenyon Whitman have been pivotal in documenting the lived experiences of Black youth in care and have provided some important links between education and foster care.

Harvey, Gupta-Kagan, and Church (2021) have identified how schools are often complicit partners in this harmful system (which they refer to as the family regulation system) and its treatment of Black students, while Whitman (2023) has documented the manner in which carceral entanglements plague Black families in harmful ways, and how the foster system is an integral part of these efforts. These works are to be applauded for their willingness to speak ugly truths about a system that is often deemed benign from those who do not have any experiences with it.

Yet through all of the challenges, some young people still thrive in a system that, some would suggest, does not always create pathways of hope and possibilities. We need to hear more of these stories of young people that defy the odds and show us what success can look like for youth in care. This is why Royel Johnson's work is needed at this moment.

The educational literature on youth in foster care has been scant at best, but it is growing. And what we know has often been situated in deficit-based accounts that document the shortcomings or failures of youth in these systems, as opposed to addressing the shortcomings of the system itself. We need more asset-based approaches that demonstrate youth persistence in what could be described as difficult systems to navigate. We need to understand more about how systems and structures that are designed to protect and care for vulnerable youth often fail in this important responsibility. We need to hear more about youth in foster care from various subgroups—namely, Black, Brown, and Indigenous youth in who have lived experiences in these systems. We also need to hear about the experiences and life challenges of LGBTQ+ youth in care, and how they are often multiply marginalized. Moreover, Transition Aged Youth (TAY) are often overlooked and underserved.

We also need to hear from those who have successfully navigated these systems. What do they say is needed from a system that fails to many of its young? What can young people who grew up in such systems offer us in the name of either reforming foster care or abolishing it altogether? What and who were critical supports along the journey?

We do not seek to lift up those youth who have overcome odds and obstacles of proof to say that the system is working, and that the responsibility of youth in the system is on them to just "do better" "work harder," or "stop making excuses." To the contrary, we should conclude that far too often the fault lies in the systems. The goal is to see young people in foster care who pursue and attain college aspirations as the norm and not the exception.

The importance of Johnson's book is that he beautifully and rigorously captures the complexity of the lives of young people in care. He centers youth voices and stories in a manner that brings us joy in seeing the promise and intellect of young people, but simultaneously provokes deep anger around systemic factors that place too many young people in such dire circumstances in the first place.

There is a need to hear from the voices of individuals with lived experiences in foster care to help us make the systems more responsive, more inclusive, and more mindful of the complexities of being in a system that purports to provide better care than children's biological families. How can we learn and replicate these supports to improve outcomes for youth in foster care?

The focus on youth in foster care needs to also pay attention to young people's multiple identities. Approaches to supporting young people in systems cannot use a one-size approach. One of the strengths of Johnson's work is that he captures how race, ethnicity, gender identity, sexual orientation, and language all matter. This book is one of the best yet on how we must do a better job of thinking about and making explicit links between foster care and college. Sadly, some estimates contend that 8–10% of youth in foster care graduate from college. There is much more that we can do for our most vulnerable young people in our nation when it comes to education opportunities. Education can and should be the proverbial equalizer that provides hope and better life chances for those seeking it. Yet for too many young people growing up in foster care, college can seem like merely a distant dream, and not a realistic goal or option.

Examining the challenges and lived experiences of youth in care and their college pursuits is vital for a number of reasons. College access continues to be elusive for many students in adverse circumstances (e.g., unhoused, foster, or incarcerated youth), but documenting the stories, struggles, and supports utilized in accessing college is informative because it informs us of what is possible, shows us how access is created, contributes to an asset-based narrative for youth in foster care, and challenges us to create a better system to support youth with college aspirations.

As we read this important book, we must remember that these young people are the exception and not the norm. We must be dedicated to fixing systems, not children and families, so that more young people, such as the 49 discussed in this book, are the norm. In these pages, you will learn about the role that dreaming, persistence, determination, support, hope, resistance, and possibility can offer young people in foster care. Royel Johnson beautifully lifts up the value of the spirit of determination in these young people and how they refuse to succumb to the narrative of what is not possible, and how they defy tremendous odds to make the seemingly impossible possible.

We should applaud the sheer brilliance, genius, and problem-solving skills of these 49 young people. But I also encourage us to think about why youth in care must always be resilient. Resilience is exhausting under normal circumstances, and even more taxing when considering young people who are facing adverse childhood experiences. It begs the question of why we only recognize the resilience of youth in care. Finding ways to be resilient in addressing and dismantling generational poverty, structural racism, mental health issues, and heteronormative patriarchy would go a long way to reducing the need for foster care systems. Taking steps to provide families with access to affordable housing and decent paying jobs that provide a livable wage would also help to reduce the need for foster care.

All too often, young people in foster care are there because of the constant manner in which the criminalization of poverty has become all too real, resulting in disproportionate numbers of Black and Brown children removed from their homes and never reunited with their families because of an inability to have basic needs met, which is unacceptable. Systems matter. Stories matter too, and Johnson has made an indelible contribution to our understanding of youth in care.

The importance of Royel Johnson's work is that he helps us to understand how system failure leads to horrific outcomes for many young people. We can be better for young people in vulnerable situations, and the power of story challenges us to increase our awareness, develop empathy, and move to action. By uplifting the stories of young people in the foster system we gain an insight into their circumstances, and hopefully it informs and inspires us to act with care, compassion, and advocacy.

—Tyrone C. Howard
UCLA

REFERENCES

Harvey, B. (2023) *Defying carceral entrapment: Black foster youth narratives of subversion, survival and liberation* [unpublished doctoral dissertation]. University of California, Los Angeles.

Harvey, B., Gupta-Kagan, J., & Church, C. (2021). Reimagining schools' role outside the family regulation system. *Columbia Journal of Race and Law, 11*(3), 575–610. https://doi.org/10.52214/cjrl.v11i3.8745

Roberts, D. E. (2001). *Shattered bonds: The color of child welfare*. Basic Books.

Roberts, D. E. (2022). *Torn apart: How the child welfare system destroys Black families—and how abolition can build a safer world*. Basic Books.

Whitman, K. L. (2023). Resisting a carceral institution: Towards supporting students with involvement in the family regulation system. *Child and Adolescent Social Work Journal, 40*, 295–297. https://doi.org/10.1007/s10560-023-00915-2

Series Foreword

In this incisive, informative, and engaging study of the journeys of 49 students from the foster care system to college, Johnson shares his powerful personal story of how the care and support of relatives saved him from the state-administered foster care system. He also describes how being a part of a family that provided care for a youth influenced his gaze and perceptions of the foster care system. The author's insightful text and absorbing stories of the students who participated in his study illuminate and document the negative and detrimental effects of the institutionalized foster care system on youths. The foster care system is especially toxic for Black and other marginalized youth of color, for LGBTQ+ youth, and especially for queer youth of color.

The problems in the institutionalized foster care system include minimal to no monitoring of host families and deficiencies in post-placement support. Some youths are placed in exploitative environments because many host families undergo little or no vetting or assessment. Serious disruptions in the education and emotional development of youth occur when they are forced to move from one placement to another. Johnson explicates why the foster care system, which in the past served primarily White youths, is now overrepresented by Black and other youths of color. Black youths are 14% of the child population but make up 22% of youths in foster care. The factors that result in youth of color being disproportionately high in foster care include the War on Drugs in the 1970s, which led to the mass incarceration of Blacks and Latinos, disrupting their family structures and resulting in many of their children being placed in the foster care system (Alexander, 2020; Stevenson, 2015). Biased reporting and investigations of child abuse and neglect have caused welfare agencies to remove children of color from their families while youths in White families with similar circumstances and characteristics remain in their families. Rather than providing stability, foster care often results in a revolving door of homes and families for many youths of color and LGBTQ+ youth. The engrossing stories conveyed by the youth who participated in this study also reveal the ways in which the negative attitudes and perceptions teachers have of youth in foster care adversely affect their school experiences.

The comprehensive ways in which this book details how institutionalized and structural racism permeates the journeys of marginalized youth of color and LGBTQ+ youth as they transition from high school to college makes it an important contribution to the Multicultural Education Series. The major purpose of the Multicultural Education Series is to provide preservice educators, practicing educators, graduate students, scholars, and policymakers with an interrelated and comprehensive set of books that summarizes and analyzes important research, theory, and practice related to the education of ethnic, racial, cultural, and linguistic groups in the United States and the education of mainstream students about diversity. The dimensions of multicultural education, developed by Banks in the *Handbook of Research on Multicultural Education* (2004) and further described in *The Routledge Companion to Multicultural Education* (Banks, 2009) and the *Encyclopedia of Diversity in Education* (Banks, 2012), provide the conceptual framework for the development of the publications in the Series. The dimensions are *content integration, the knowledge construction process, prejudice reduction, equity pedagogy*, and an *empowering institutional culture and social structure.*

The books in the Multicultural Education Series provide research, theoretical, and practical knowledge about the behaviors and learning characteristics of students of color (Darling-Hammond & Darling-Hammond, 2022; Conchas & Vigil, 2012; Lee, 2007), language minority students (Gándara & Hopkins 2010; Valdés, 2001; Valdés et al., 2011), low-income students (Cookson, 2013; Gorski, 2018), and other minoritized population groups, such as students who speak different varieties of English (Charity Hudley & Mallinson, 2011), LGBTQ+ youth (Mayo, 2022), and students with disabilities (Waitoller & Thorius, 2022).

A number of books in the Multicultural Education Series focus on *institutional and structural racism* and ways to reduce it in educational institutions. These books include Özlem Sensoy and Robin DiAngelo (2017), *Is Everyone Really Equal? An Introduction to Key Concepts in Social Justice Education* (Second Edition); Gary Howard (2016), *We Can't Teach What We Don't Know: White Teachers, Multiracial Schools* (Third Edition); Jabari Mahiri (2017), *Deconstructing Race: Multicultural Education Beyond the Color-Bind;* Zeus Leonardo (2013), *Race Frameworks: A Multidimensional Theory of Racism and Education*; *Racial Microaggressions: Using Critical Race Theory in Education to Recognize and Respond to Everyday Racism* by Daniel Solórzano and Lindsay Pérez Huber (2020), and *Seeing Whiteness: The Essential Essays of Robin DiAngelo* (2023).

This book chronicles the lives and experience of 49 youths in foster care who are navigating the challenging terrain to attend college. Other books in the Multicultural Education Series describe problems related to diversity in higher education and ways in which it can be reformed. These books include *Engaging the "Race Question": Accountability and Equity in U. S. Higher Education* by Alicia C. Dowd and Estela Mara Bensimon (2015); *Race, Empire, and English Language Teaching: Creating Responsible and Ethical Anti-Racist Practice* by Suhanthie Motha (2014); *Achieving Equity for Latino Students: Expanding the Pathway to Higher Education Through Public Policy* by Frances Contreras (2011); *Americans by Heart: Undocumented Latino Students and the Promise of Higher Education* by William Pèrez (2011); *Asians in the Ivory Tower: Dilemmas of Racial Inequality in American Higher Education* by Robert T. Teranishi (2010); *Immigrant-Origin Students in Community College: Navigating Risk and Reward in Higher Education,* edited by Carola Suárez-Orozco and Olivia Osei-Twumasi (2019); *Campus Uprisings: How Student Activists and Collegiate Leaders Resist Racism and Create Hope*, edited by Ty-Ron M. O. Douglas, Kmt G. Shockley, and Ivory Toldson (2020); and *Whiteness in the Ivory Tower: Why Don't We Notice the White Students Sitting Together in the Quad?* by Nolan L. Cabrera (2024).

Despite the challenges they experience in the institutionalized foster care system, Johnson illuminates and details the self-reliance and resiliency the youth in his study exemplified, which he describes as stories of "resilience, determination, and agency" (Chapter 2, p. 29). He writes, "[Like] Cedric and myself, they possess a relentless drive and an unwavering hope—a hope often unseen by those around them" (Chapter 3, p. 31). Johnson continues, "Therefore, I argue that youth of color in foster care can and often do maintain high hopes for college despite barriers because they come from cultural communities where an orientation toward hope is highly valued. These communities instill the importance of identifying multiple paths and strategies to overcome obstacles" (Chapter 3, p. 40).

Johnson details the problems with the institutionalized foster care system but also describes actions and reforms that can be taken by policymakers, administrators, and other stakeholders to improve it and to enrich the lives of youth in foster care. The voices and concerns of youth in foster care regarding their placement and education should be recognized, validated, and heard. Teacher education should include components that help teachers develop positive attitudes and perceptions of youth in foster care and to understand how trauma, school disruptions, and bullying affect their lives. Youth in foster care should also be provided knowledge about early college awareness and preparation programs and initiatives that cater to their needs. Helping youth in foster care deal with housing insecurity as they transition from foster care to colleges and universities is essential. Johnson details how San Francisco State University has dealt with housing insecurity creatively and effectively by providing year-round housing for students transitioning from foster care to college.

Youth who have experienced foster care tell cogent, riveting, and inspirational stories in this timely, powerful, captivating—and at times poignant—book. It is an important and singular addition to the Multicultural Education Series. I hope this book will receive the warm reception and serious deliberation by readers that it richly deserves.

—James A. Banks

REFERENCES

Alexander, M. (2020). *The new Jim Crow: Mass incarceration in the age of colorblindness.* The New Press.

Banks, J. A. (2004). Multicultural education: Historical development, dimensions, and practice. In J. A. Banks & C. A. M. Banks (Eds.), *Handbook of research on multicultural education* (2nd ed., pp. 3–29). Jossey-Bass.

Banks, J. A. (Ed.). (2009). *The Routledge international companion to multicultural education.* Routledge.

Banks, J. A. (2012). Multicultural education: Dimensions of. In J. A. Banks (Ed.), *Encyclopedia of diversity in education* (vol. 3, pp. 1538–1547). Sage Publications.

Cabrera, N. L. (2024). *Whiteness in the ivory tower: Why don't we notice the White students sitting together in the quad?* Teachers College Press.

Charity Hudley, A. H., & Mallinson, C. (2011). *Understanding language variation in U.S. schools.* Teachers College Press.

Conchas, G. Q., & Vigil, J. D. (2012). *Streetsmart schoolsmart: Urban poverty and the education of adolescent boys.* Teachers College Press.

Contreras, F. (2011). *Achieving equity for Latino students: Expanding the pathway to higher education through public policy.* Teachers College Press.

Cookson, P. W., Jr. (2013). *Class rules: Exposing inequality in American high schools.* Teachers College Press.

DiAngelo, R. (2023). *Seeing whiteness: The essential essays of Robin DiAngelo.* Teachers College Press.

Darling-Hammond, K., & Darling-Hammond, L. (2022). *The civil rights road to deeper learning: Five essentials for equity.* Teachers College Press.

Douglas, T. -R, Shockley, K. G., & Toldson, I. (Eds). (2020). *Campus uprisings: How student activists and collegiate leaders resist racism and create hope.* Teachers College Press.

Dowd, A. C., & Bensimon, E. M. (2015). *Engaging the "race question:" Accountability and equity in U.S. higher education.* Teachers College Press.

Gándara, P., & Hopkins, M. (Eds.). (2010). *Forbidden language: English language learners and restrictive language policies*. Teachers College Press.
Gorski, P. C. (2018). *Reaching and teaching students in poverty: Strategies for erasing the opportunity gap* (2nd ed.). Teachers College Press.
Howard, G. (2016). *We can't teach what we don't know: White teachers, multiracial schools* (3rd ed.). Teachers College Press.
Lee, C. D. (2007). *Culture, literacy, and learning: Taking bloom in the midst of the whirlwind*. Teachers College Press.
Leonardo, Z. (2013). *Race frameworks: A multidimensional theory of racism and education*. Teachers College Press.
Mahiri, J. (2017). *Deconstructing race: Multicultural education beyond the color-bind*. Teachers College Press.
Mayo, C. (2022). *LGBTQ youth and education: Policies and practices*. Teachers College Press.
Motha, S. (2014). *Race, empire and English language teaching: Creating responsible and ethical anti-racist practice*. Teachers College Press.
Pérez, W. (2011). *Americans by heart: Undocumented Latino students and the promise of higher education*. Teachers College Press.
Sensoy, Ö., & DiAngelo, R. (2017). *Is everyone really equal? An introduction to key concepts in social justice education* (2nd ed.). Teachers College Press.
Solórzano, D., & Huber, L. P. (2020). *Racial microaggressions: Using critical race theory to respond to everyday racism*. Teachers College Press.
Stevenson, B. (2015). *Just mercy: A story of justice and redemption*. One World.
Suárez-Orozco, C., & Osei-Twumasi, O. (2019). *Immigrant-origin students in community college: Navigating risk and reward in higher education*. Teachers College Press.
Teranishi, R. T. (2010). *Asians in the ivory tower: Dilemmas of racial inequality in American higher education*. Teachers College Press.
Valdés, G. (2001). *Learning and not learning English: Latino Students in American schools*. Teachers College Press.
Valdés, G., Capitelli, S., & Alvarez, L. (2011). *Latino children learning English: Steps in the journey*. Teachers College Press.
Waitoller, F. R., & Thorius, K. A. K. (2022). *Sustaining disabled youth: Centering disability in asset pedagogies*. Teachers College Press.

Acknowledgments

No feat like this is ever accomplished alone. Although the words in this book are mine, they were brought to life with the invaluable support of an expansive community.

First and foremost, thank you to the students who invited me into their worlds amid a global pandemic. I have tried my best to take care in telling your stories and will continue to commit my career to improving the material conditions of our most underserved groups. Special thanks also to those who served in an advisory capacity, providing tremendous insight and guidance throughout the life of this project.

I am profoundly grateful to my research team—Allante Moon, Gabriel Pulido, Bridget Parler, and Gabriel Kim. Their enthusiasm and curiosity for the project were essential in getting this work off the ground. I am especially thankful for Allante, now Dr. Moon, for her diligence, hard work, and leadership as the lead graduate assistant. Her contributions were instrumental.

This project experienced many starts and stops. When I received the contract for this book in December 2020, amid the global COVID-19 pandemic, I could not have imagined what was to come shortly after. At that time, I was only 3 years into my faculty career and soon found myself preparing for early promotion and tenure, relocating across the country to the University of Southern California, and dealing with a significant familial loss. Suffice it to say, I was burned out.

There were moments when I considered abandoning this project. I made numerous unfulfilled promises to deliver a draft manuscript to my editors. Despite these setbacks, they extended tremendous grace, kindness, and patience. For this, I am eternally grateful to Brian Ellerbeck and Jim Banks. Jim, it is an honor to have my first sole-authored book included in your storied Multicultural Education Series. I eagerly anticipate partnering with you and Brian on my next project.

They say "it takes a village," and I know for sure that it isn't just hyperbole. Indeed, it has taken a village. Allow me a moment to express gratitude to my extensive and supportive village. Thank you to my doctoral advisor and friend, Terrell Strayhorn, for role-modeling what it means to be a serious interdisciplinary scholar. As I have said publicly so many times before, any good that has come out of my career is a result of the considerable personal and professional investments you have made in me. Thank you.

Thank you to my late aunt Priscilla Ann Echols, whom I lost as I was completing this book. An author of many books herself, she was the first author I knew. As a kid, she invited me into her writing process, helping her to develop characters and storylines, and giving feedback on what eventually became her novel, *Consequences*. "Auntie Ann," as I affectionately called her, I cherish every moment we shared. In our last conversations before you transitioned, I promised you I would finish this book and would continue to use my voice. I hope I have made you proud.

As I was managing what felt like unbearable grief following my aunt's untimely transition, there was a bright light that came into my life, one that helped me to gather my bearings and begin to find the strength to persist: Marquelle Turner-Gilchrist. MTG, thank you for your, support, accountability, and sometimes reprimand. No one checked in with me more about the status of my writing and progress than you. I am eternally grateful for you.

To everyone who entertained a conversation with me about my work; stood in the gap in some way, shape, or form; or who just sent good vibes my way, thank you. This includes my immediate family, mom (Mona), dad (Roy), sister (Raven), aunt (Mary), cousin (Tonia), stepdad (Keith), as well as the following (alphabetical order): Aerian Brown, Ahja Steele, Alicia Dowd, Ali Watts, Alex Kenney, Aramie Payton, Aryn Terry, Adrianna Kezar, Brian Burt, Brian McGowan, Brittney Cleveland, Brendesha Tynes, Cameron Beatty, Chelsea Hayes, Chris Emdin, Christian Lochan, Christopher Benson, Darnell Moore, Danielle LaVaque-Manty, Derrick Brooms, Dominic Bednar, Dorien Blythers, Eddie Cole, Eboni Zamani Gallagher, Ericka Weathers, Felecia Commodore, Francesca Lopez, Gil Conchas, Imani Amos, Ivory Berry, James Earl Davis, Jennifer Geiger, Jeffrey Pugh, Jessica Decuir-Gunby, Joy Gaston Gayles, Julia Bryan, Julie Posselt, Kaleb Briscoe, Karla Zaccor, Karly Ford, Keenan Thompson, Kelly Rosinger, Kendrick Davis, Kim Lawless, LaWanda Ward, Leonard Taylor, Liliana Garces, Lorenzo Baber, Maria Lewis, Marcus Bragg, Marsha Modeste, Maddy Day, Michael Harden, Milagra Ward, Montrischa Williams, Nathanael Okpych, Nolan Cabrera, Randy Bonds, Rachel Brown, Rachelle Winkle-Wagner, Riana Anderson, Roland Pope, Roman Liera, Sam Prater, Shaun Harper, Shawn Hill, Steven Jefferson, T'Chana Bradford, Tiffany Squires, William Edmond, William Trent, Wilson Okello, Yvonne Unrau, and Zoe Corwin.

This by no means represents an exhaustive list. If I have inadvertently failed to mention your name, please forgive me. Know that I am thankful and grateful for your support.

Thank you, thank you, thank you.

From Foster Care to College

CHAPTER 1

Introduction

What does it mean to truly belong? To have a place that anchors you, supports you, and positively shapes the very essence of who you become? For many students, this foundation is a taken-for-granted given—a home, a family, a stable education. But what happens when these constants are shaken, shifted, or shattered altogether? When "home" is an ever-changing and often unsafe context, and school, instead of being a "safe haven" for learning, development, and growth, is sometimes a site of oppression and marginalization?

How do young people in the foster care system navigate an education system ill-equipped to address their unique needs? Where do they find their reservoirs of resilience when faced with frequent, unwarranted transitions and interruptions? And more importantly, how does our nation, a supposed bastion of hope and opportunity, allow these problems to persist, marginalizing some of its most vulnerable youth?

For the nearly 400,000 young people in the foster care system, these are not rhetorical questions but visceral realities. The stories of students you will encounter in this book—from NiQi and Doc Mills to Barbie and others—are often relegated to the margins and silenced in the national discourse on college access and student success, but they evince hope, resistance, and possibility despite challenges. In this book, I amplify their narratives, exposing the systemic challenges they face, and more crucially, the undying spirit that propels them forward. But first, allow me to offer some context.

SETTING THE STAGE

The foster care system is touted as a protective intervention for young people who experience, or are suspected of experiencing, abuse or neglect. Its mission is to provide safe and temporary out-of-home care, with the goal of reunifying children and youth with their families. Yet, for youth in the foster care system, data tell a different story.

According to the Adoption and Foster Care Analysis and Reporting System (AFCARS), which provides publicly available national data to aid in policy development and program management, the average age of children in the foster care is roughly 8 years old. Additionally, the notion that foster care is "temporary" is challenged by the fact that, on average, these young people spend about 22 months—almost 2 years—in the system (U.S. Department of Health and Human Sciences, 2021).

That the foster care system mirrors deep-seated societal inequities may not come as a surprise. Black youth, who constitute only 14% of the total child population, are disproportionately represented in the foster care system, accounting for 22% of those in care. Similarly, American Indian and Alaska Native children, while only 1% of the child population in the United States, are double that figure, 2%, in the foster care system (U.S. Department of Health and Human Sciences, 2021). The reasons for these disparities are complex. Suffice it to say that racism permeates the child welfare system as it does all other social systems in the United States.

While reunification with family is the primary case goal for most youth in care, approximately 20,000 still "age out" of the foster system each year (U.S. Department of Health and Human Sciences, 2021). It used to be the case that this transition occurred when they turned 18 years old; however, growing awareness about the challenges of youth in foster care and successful lobbying have led most states to extend foster care services to the ages of 19, 20, 21, and older (see Figure 1.1; Child Welfare Information Gateway, 2022). Among those aging out, Black youth are overrepresented, and as a result, experience greater risk of homelessness, incarceration, teen pregnancy, and challenges completing school (KIDS Count, 2020). Extended foster care, however, can act as a protective factor for young people, allowing them additional time to develop life skills, nurture relationships, and access important resources necessary for education and employment (Courtney, Okpych, & Park, 2018).

The reasons that young people in foster care experience difficulties completing school are complex. Research has shown that the very act of placement in foster care can be deeply traumatic for youth, as it means loss or separation from their biological family, friends, and community (Papovich, 2020). This trauma, when combined with any prior experiences of abuse or neglect, can manifest in learning disabilities and emotional and behavioral disorders, leading to special education placements. A study by Scherr (2007) underscores this disparity: 31% of youth in foster care qualify for special education services, in stark comparison to the national average of 13% for all students.

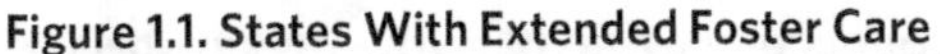

Figure 1.1. States With Extended Foster Care

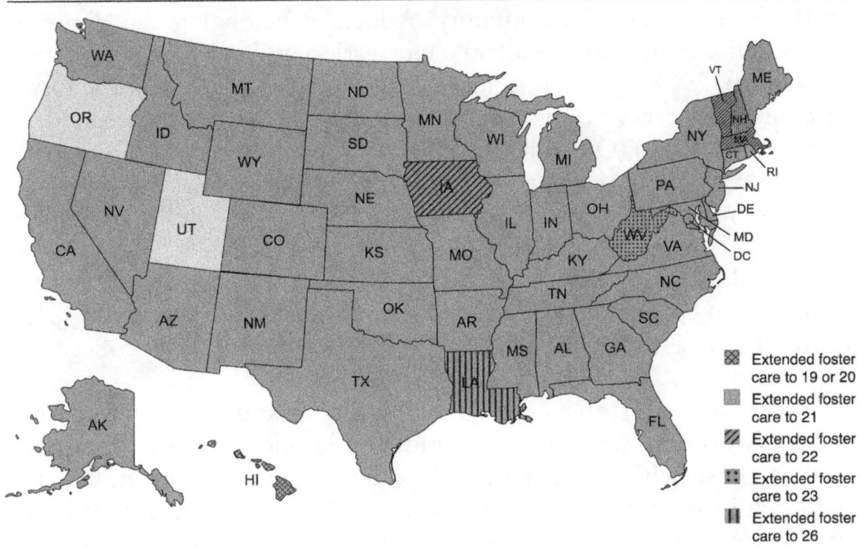

Further complicating matters is the fact that the longer young people spend in foster care, the more residential placement changes they experience (James, 2004; Konijn et al., 2019). Each change often results in school transfer, disrupting not only educational continuity but also the development of supportive relationships with peers, teachers, and staff—folks who could otherwise serve as stable support sources (Johnson et al., 2020). The impact of these challenges intensifies when coordination between child welfare agencies and school administration is lacking, resulting in delays in transferring school records and subsequent enrollment.

Teachers can also play a significant role in these challenges, and not always positively. Consider the fact that roughly one in five American adults report having little to no knowledge about the foster care system (National CASA, 2009). Consequently, many educators may be unaware of or ill-equipped to address the unique needs of youth in care. Even worse, some may even hold negative stereotypes about these youths that influence their interactions and level of commitment to them. Unfortunately, stereotypes that paint youth in foster care as incorrigible and deviant are all too common.

While school might serve as a home away from home or a "safe haven" for some youth, these cumulative challenges can collectively act as barriers to experiencing a sense of school belonging (Johnson et al., 2020)—that is, feeling connected to, a part of, and respected by the broader school community. A lack of belonging can diminish student engagement and academic motivation and can lead to attrition (Strayhorn, 2018). Thus, it is not entirely surprising that youth in foster care lag their peers in high school completion, as well postsecondary access and success (Okpych, 2022).

The data are both clear and troubling. Though upward of 70–80% of youth in foster care aspire to graduate from college, fewer anticipate turning this aspiration into reality (Courtney, Terao, & Bost, 2004; Kirk et al., 2013; Okpych et al., 2015). The most reliable evidence available on college enrollment and degree completion rates for youth in foster care estimates that about 8–10% ultimately earn college degrees (Okpych, 2021; Okpych et al., 2021).

Grim as these statistics may be, the stories and experiences of the 8–10% who defy seemingly insurmountable odds to earn degrees, as well as those who make it to college but don't complete it, are rife with rich insights and are worthy of close study. Their stories of hope, often unseen, alongside tales of possibility and resistance in the face of systemic challenges, provide an invaluable lens through which we can identify and understand both the failings of our systems and what hard work lies ahead to enable their success. It is for this reason that I decided to write this book.

PURPOSE AND SCOPE

From Foster Care to College is a sensitive yet critical exploration of the lived experiences of 49 students as they navigate their journey through the foster care system and the challenges of higher education. Through in-depth life story interviews, this book not only sheds light on the harsh realities these young people face but also provides insights into how our nation's education and child welfare systems collaborate in ways that limit these youths' potential and opportunities (Johnson, 2021).

But this narrative isn't singularly about hardship; it's a multifaceted story rich with threads of hope, resistance, and possibility. Anchored by resilience theory, *From Foster Care to College* sheds light on the protective mechanisms and inherent strengths that facilitate postsecondary access and success amid the systems' failures.

More than an exposition, it's a clarion call to educators, school and university leaders, and child welfare advocates to stand tall and take decisive action. My goal is simple: to transform the precarious circumstances of young people in foster care, dismantling the barriers that hinder their educational pursuits and dreams. My wish is that the stories shared in these chapters not only move you but also inspire transformative action within your sphere of influence that significantly improves the material conditions of those in the system.

CONCEPTUAL SCAFFOLDING

While the methodological details are included in the appendix, allow me to share information about the broad conceptual framework that underpins this research. In line with Eve Tuck's (2009) call to eschew damage-centered research, *From Foster Care to College* unequivocally rejects narratives that imprison young people in foster care within frames of brokenness and deficiency. This work conscientiously navigates between exposing the glaring inequities of systemic structures and underscoring the beautiful spirit, hope, and agency reflected in their journeys.

The conceptual and theoretical scaffold of this project is firmly anchored within liberatory and humanizing perspectives (Savage et al., 2021), with both serving distinctive yet complementary roles in framing the stories presented within these pages.

Humanizing research, as defined in this book, is more than a theoretical and methodological stance; it is an ethical commitment. Predicated on nurturing relationships of care and dignity among researchers and participants, this approach ensures that the narratives unfold within a space where voices are not only heard but honored and respected. It fosters an environment where stories, in all their pain and triumph, are handled with respect and care.

Likewise, a liberatory research lens seeks to emancipate, amplifying narratives that transcend prescriptive narratives of pain and deficit. Freedom-focused, liberatory research acknowledges both the individual and communal worth of students, emancipating them, and by extension, their stories, from narratives of hopelessness that have long permeated educational discourse.

These frames work in tandem as the conceptual umbrella for this work. Also anchoring it is resilience theory. Resilience refers to the successful adaption of an individual, in this case a student, despite their exposure to adversity (Fergus & Zimmerman, 2005). Successful adaption is often defined from an outcome's perspective, such as high school graduation and postsecondary education enrollment, which was certainly of interest to me in this project. Equally important, however, are the self-defined goals that young people in foster care set and accomplish for themselves. Adversity encompasses risk factors like child abuse or neglect that can undermine successful adaption.

In this research, I focus on "resilient youth" with foster care experience who have actively engaged in education and successfully completed traditional benchmarks such high school graduation, college application and transition, matriculation, and for some, college degree completion. In addition, considering risk factors that contribute to educational failure, I widen the aperture to account for protective factors, both internal and external, that enable successful adaption (Fergus & Zimmerman, 2005). Internal factors, or *assets*, refer to individual-level qualities or characteristics such as one's skills, attitudes, beliefs, dispositions, or values. External factors, or *resources*, "are the environmental supports and opportunities available in the home, school, community, and peer groups" (Gizir & Aydin, 2009, p. 39). These may include caring relationships, high and positive expectations, and participation in meaningful activities.

While the broad strokes of this conceptual framework shape the overarching narrative of *From Foster Care to College*, it is important to note that some chapters will delve into other theories related to the themes being explored. These focused explorations, while nested within the wider frame, allow for a nuanced, in-depth analysis, ensuring each story is honored in its rich, multifaceted entirety.

THE STUDENTS

The research that informs this book includes 49 diverse students who brought a wide range of experiences and important dimensions of social identity into focus. Here is some crucial demographic and background information about them:

- *Ethnicity and Race:* The students exhibited diversity in terms of their ethnic and racial backgrounds. The breakdown includes 16 White students, 15 Black students, 9 Latinx students, 5 multiracial students, and 4 Asian/Pacific Islander students.
- *Gender:* Most of the students identified as cisgender women (33), while 14 were cisgender men, 1 identified as nonbinary, and 1 as a trans woman.
- *Sexual Orientation:* Most of the students identified as heterosexual (30). Nine students identified as bisexual, 3 as gay, 3 as pansexual, 3 as lesbian, and 1 as queer.
- *Age:* The students' ages spanned a wide range, indicating a diverse group that included adult learners. The youngest student was 18 years old, while the oldest was 41.

- *Enrollment Status:* Almost all the students were currently enrolled in higher education, with 2 being graduate students. Those not enrolled were recent college graduates.
- *Undergraduate Institution:* Most students in the sample attended 4-year colleges and universities (88%), with the remaining 12% attending 2-year community colleges.
- *Year in School:* Among the surveyed students, 20% were in their freshman/1st year, 27% were sophomores/2nd year, 18% were junior/3rd-year students, 20% were seniors/5 or more years into their college journey, and 4% were graduate students.
- *Major:* The academic majors among the 49 students were diverse. The most prevalent major was social work, with 18% of students majoring in it. Other prominent categories included social sciences (16%), natural sciences (16%), and fine arts and human services and health-related majors (both at 12%). Additionally, 8% majored in business and finance, 4% in communication and media or computer science and technology, and another 4% in legal studies and criminal justice. A smaller portion, 2%, studied mathematics and philosophy, showcasing the variety of academic disciplines represented among the students.
- *High School GPA (HS GPA) and College GPA:* Our analysis of the students' academic performance revealed a range of GPAs. The median high school GPA was 3.40, while the median college GPA was 3.00. Additionally, the average high school GPA was 3.24, and the average college GPA was 3.12. These figures provide insight into the academic achievements of our participants and their transition to higher education.
- *Foster Care Experience:* The data on time spent in foster care and residential placement changes revealed a wide range of experiences among the individuals. The duration in foster care varied from as short as 1 year to over 20 years, with a substantial portion having spent 9 to 10 years in care. Residential placement changes also varied significantly, with some individuals having experienced as few as one placement change and others enduring over 100 changes, according to their accounts. Moreover, 51% "aged-out" of foster care. These numbers underscore the diversity and complexity of the students' journeys through the foster care system.
- *School Placement Changes:* The data on school placement changes among the students indicated a wide range of experiences. Some students reported having changed schools

frequently, with numbers exceeding 10 changes in some cases. Conversely, a few students mentioned having experienced no school changes at all. The variability in school placement changes emphasizes the challenges and disruptions these students may face in their education.

- *Incarceration History:* Out of the students in the sample, approximately 28% had experienced periods of incarceration, while the remaining 72% did not have any involvement with incarceration.

It's important to note that the demographic data mentioned above were all self-reported by the students.

MORE THAN AN INTELLECTUAL EXERCISE: MY JOURNEY TO THIS WORK

This research is deeply personal. It is more than an intellectual exercise or underexamined subject to be explored—it is a world that I have, in part, navigated personally. Before we delve into the stories of the students who are the focus of this research, allow me a moment to turn inward, to share how I arrived at the project that is the basis for this book.

Family matters. This lesson was imparted to me early in life. During a difficult chapter in my mother's journey, which limited her ability to care for me, my sister and I found care, love, and stability through my biological family, particularly my aunt Priscilla, whose memory I honor and dedicate this book to—may she rest in peace.

The continuity of care that my aunt and others provided during this difficult time fundamentally altered the trajectory of my life. It meant that my sister and I were spared from formal involvement with the foster care system. This experience is known as informal kinship care (Gleeson et al., 2009), where a relative steps in to provide temporary care, safeguarding the children from the turmoil that often accompanies formal system involvement. Such intervention, in my case, shielded us from the scrutiny of Child Protective Services—an interaction that, for Black families like mine, seldom results in favorable outcomes.

A bit later in life, when things were more stable at home, my cousin came to stay with us. A middle schooler at the time, she had already spent several years in foster care, residing with a godmother who was unfit to provide her safety and care.

I still vividly recall the day the child welfare caseworker brought her to our house. We had spent the weekend meticulously preparing for their visit, cleaning every corner in anticipation of the caseworker's inspection to determine whether our home was suitable. At that time, my mother, toddler sister, and I lived in a very modest one-bedroom apartment on the West Side of Chicago. I was about 9 years old. Our bedroom included a full-size bed for my mom and sister and a two-tiered bunk bed that would now house my cousin and me.

My cousin stayed with us for a few years. During this time, I had a front row seat to the glaring shortcomings and outright failures of our systems, including both child welfare and education—her struggles with initial placements, aging out of the system and transitioning to independent living (a period during which she became a teen mother), and bouts with homelessness and persistent instability.

My near entrance into the foster care system, coupled with my experience being part of a family that provided care for a youth within it, has indelibly shaped my life and perceptions of the system. It planted a seed of advocacy and intellectual curiosity within me that would lay dormant for many years. It wasn't until my transition into academia, specifically during my doctoral studies, that this latent seed found fertile ground in which to take root.

While at Ohio State, I became part of a research team, guided by my doctoral advisor, that afforded me the opportunity to formally delve into the study of these issues. In the decade since, I have devoted scholarly attention to the educational experiences and outcomes of young people in foster care, but more importantly, I have also been an advocate for improving their material conditions.

I share this context to illuminate the deeply personal foundation upon which this work is based. My journey, though different from that of those who graciously invited my team and me into their world, has considerably influenced my work, and certainly every page contained within this book. It is through this prism—shaped by lived experience, observation, and advocacy—that I entered and approached this work, navigating with care, respect, and an unwavering commitment to equity and justice.

READING *FROM FOSTER CARE TO COLLEGE*

This research was designed to elicit comprehensive insights about the lived experiences of young people in foster care, from their journeys through its system, navigating K–12 education and postsecondary education, and to the joys and challenges of fashioning their own futures. Throughout the following chapters, we will "zoom in" on several focal students and their stories to provide more rich, nuanced accounts, while also "zooming out" to more thematically capture the experiences that resonate across the broader cohort in the sample.

As I mentioned earlier in the introduction, the child welfare system, and the educational implications for young people with foster care experience, often lack public awareness. *From Foster Care to College* aims to help bridge the gap by shedding light on both the systemic obstacles and the resilience that characterize the experiences of these youth. My wish is that it challenges prevailing narratives and offers new perspectives that are critical for informing effective policy and practice.

This research is not just an academic exercise; it is a call to action for educators, policymakers, and society at large to recognize and address the educational needs and aspirations of youth in the foster care system. It is an effort to ensure that these young people are no longer invisible in our educational discourse and policy planning but are acknowledged as capable, resilient individuals with the potential to succeed in higher education and beyond.

Significance

From Foster Care to College is an important and timely contribution, offering insight into the educational path for young people impacted by the foster care system. At the onset, it challenges the often-assumed benevolence the child welfare system, which espouses a commitment to protect our most vulnerable youth. It exposes the uncomfortable truth that, often, the very system meant to safeguard young people is the source of their harm.

Given the dearth of theoretically grounded research attending to the college-going experiences of young people in foster care, this book is poised to make an important contribution to knowledge. Several years ago, I conducted and published a systematic literature review on this topic (Johnson, 2021)—a companion review to my friend and colleague Jennifer Geiger's review (Geiger & Beltran, 2019), published in a social services journal. One takeaway from my review is that despite a surge in empirical studies over the past 15 years, that work remains largely atheoretical, with race and power evasive in their analysis. *From Foster Care to College* responds to this gap, attending to identity-based nuances, where possible, and leveraging assets-based theories that help shed light on students' strengths rather than deficits.

I also take great pride in the rich qualitative approach of *From Foster Care to College*. My colleagues Jacob Gross (2019) and Nathaniel Okpych (2021) have previously devoted scholarly attention to the postsecondary education experiences and outcomes of young people in foster care in their books, relying on various quantitative surveys.

These works are important in helping to capture statistical patterns of educational challenges and protective measures with relatively large sample sizes. However, *From Foster Care to College* distinguishes itself through its critical qualitative lens, offering a depth of understanding and an exploration of the nuanced, lived experiences of these remarkable individuals. It is their voices that take center stage, making them the heart of the narrative. Through their stories, we explore the very essence of resilience, resistance, and possibility.

From Foster Care to College also seeks to challenge the myopic focus on those who age out of the foster care system, which has been a central focus of past research. To be sure, such focus has been warranted given the heightened vulnerabilities youth who age out experience. However, *From Foster Care to College* broadens the focus to account for a wide range of experiences of those in care, recognizing that any time spent can have traumatic and far-reaching consequences for an individual's educational journey.

It is also important to acknowledge that past research has had a very narrow focus on risk factors, which can inadvertently pathologize youth in foster care, overlooking the systemic and structural forces that shape their lives. By widening the aperture to encompass those with varying degrees of experience and contact with the foster care system, we are able see a far more complex and comprehensive picture of the experiences and factors, both good and bad, that shape the lives of these young people.

Moreover, *From Foster Care to College* delves into the often-overlooked dimensions of identity and intersectionality, shedding light on how one's identities position them within a broader matrix of multiple and intersecting systems of oppression. Indeed, much past research in this area is race-evasive and neglects to turn attention to broader systemic forces. *From Foster Care to College* addresses these gaps.

My ultimate hope and wish is that *From Foster Care to College* is used as a powerful tool for advocacy and change that improves their material conditions by demanding accountability of systems and offering hope for youth and educators. This book ultimately invites readers to engage with the lived experiences of young people in foster care, recognizing their potential, acknowledging their struggles, and advocating for a more equitable future.

Audience

This book is intended for a diverse readership. Educators, social workers, policymakers, and advocates, I hope, will find valuable insights about the lived experiences of students that may inform and sharpen their professional practices and decisions. Students who share similar experiences and backgrounds may see reflections of their own stories, finding both solace and perhaps inspiration. Additionally, general readers with commitments to social justice and education will likely be deeply moved and educated by these compelling stories. Ultimately, *From Foster Care to College* is a testament to resilience, hope, and the transformative power of storytelling, resonating with anyone who believes in the potential of every individual, regardless of their start.

PERSON-CENTERED LANGUAGE: A NOTE ABOUT TERMS

Before I turn to the students and their stories in the following chapter, allow me a moment to reflect briefly on my choice of terminology in this book. By now, you have likely noticed that I do not use the term or label "foster youth." This is intentional. The terms we use to describe young individuals in or affected by the foster care system hold significant weight. They shape imagery, impart meaning, and can influence both positive and negative outcomes in these youths' lives. For example, the label "foster youth" might unintentionally suggest that the characteristics of these individuals are inherently linked to their foster care status (Gross, 2019). This perspective overlooks external factors like environment and circumstances that play crucial roles. Similarly, phrases such as "foster care alumni" may inadvertently imply a definitive end to the foster care experience, as if one "graduates" from it (Gross, 2019), or suggest an expiration date on this life chapter (Whitman, 2016).

In this text, I use "youth (or students) in foster care," "youth impacted by foster care," "youth with foster care experience," or some related variation. This wording is intentional and reflects a deep commitment to person-first language, recognizing the powerful impact of language on perception and treatment. This terminology aims to respect and acknowledge the individual experiences and identities of these youth, steering clear of generalizations and stereotypes. My word choices are a small but significant step toward a more inclusive and empathetic understanding of those affected by foster care.

CHAPTER OVERVIEW

Chapter 2, "System Failure: Navigating and Resisting Foster Care," delves into the chronic systemic failures of the foster care system, despite its purported aims and goals. By amplifying the narratives of students, it illuminates how they navigate and endure the challenges of this flawed system—from frequent placement changes to experiences of abuse and neglect while in care. Yet, against these odds, their stories show remarkable resilience. Through their narratives, we witness their resistance to the system's limitations and the forging of their own paths. By understanding their experiences, we gain profound insights into both the system's deficiencies and the indomitable spirit of those it encompasses.

In the third chapter, "'Hope in the Unseen': Navigating K–12 Education and Fostering College Dreams," I describe how young people with foster care experience form and maintain their dreams of college attainment despite a host of challenges that would otherwise deter and alter their educational trajectories. Yet this resilient group activates often undervalued forms of capital, relies on a constellation of protective factors, and harnesses hope to propel them forward toward their goal of college.

Chapter 4, "Choosing College as a Matter of Belonging," delves into the complex process of postsecondary enrollment decision-making. Drawing on the concept of a sense of belonging as a motivational framework, I show how students in foster care are guided by their fundamental desire to identify college campuses that are psychologically and physically safe and supportive of their identities. Moreover, I also explore the support structures that help facilitate a successful transition to their college of choice.

In Chapter 5, "'Bridges' to Postsecondary Retention, Persistence, and Completion," I turn attention to the bridges, rather than barriers, that enable students to persist and thrive academically. From the salience of one's foster and racial identity development to the critical role of financial literacy and independence, this chapter helps educators imagine how they might fashion their institutional policies and practices in ways that better serve young people.

The closing chapter synthesizes major findings and conclusions from the volume, providing a clarion call to action for educators, child welfare professionals, and other concerned actors. Indeed, in that chapter, I underscore the importance of an equity-minded stance among those poised to improve the material conditions of young people in care via policy and practice reform. Poignant recommendations are provided.

CHAPTER 2

System Failure: Navigating and Resisting Foster Care

On Tuesday, April 20, at approximately 5:30 P.M., like many around the world, I waited anxiously as the jury pronounced Derrick Chauvin guilty for the murder of George Floyd. The relief was short-lived. Just moments after, I came across the news of another tragic event—the death of 16-year-old Ma'Khia Bryant. Ma'Khia, a Black girl under foster care, was fatally shot by Columbus City Police Officer, Nicholas Reardon, during a physical altercation (Johnson, 2021).

This incident struck close to home. Before joining the faculty at Pennsylvania State University in 2017, I resided in Columbus, Ohio. During that time, I worked at The Ohio State University and collaborated extensively with Franklin County Children Services—the very agency responsible for Ma'Khia and her sister's care. Needless to say, I was very familiar with the locale where this heartbreaking tragedy transpired (Johnson, 2021).

As details about the case emerged, several unsettling details came to light. Reports suggest that leading up to Ma'Khia's tragic murder, there had been multiple 911 calls highlighting safety concerns at her residence. One of those came from Ma'Khia's sister just 23 days prior to her death. She communicated to the dispatcher: "I want to leave this foster home." When officers said they could not move her out of the house, the report indicates that she "became irate and stated that if she does not leave, then she was going to kill someone in the home." She was subsequently taken to a hospital for a psychological evaluation at the request of her foster mother, according to the incident report. Another concerning police call came from Ma'Khia's foster mom, who indicated that she was shot at while driving a car several miles from the house. This offers some context about the safety of the neighborhood Ma'Khia lived in. There were also past reported calls about missing youth who resided there under the care of Ma'Khia's foster mom, signaling significant issues with her placement in this home (Sanchez et al., 2021).

This leads one to question: How could a system that aims to protect neglected and abused children oversee their well-being so negligently that it culminated in Ma'Khia's death? The truth is that the foster care system failed Ma'Khia and her sister by allowing them to stay in an obviously unfit residential placement. And, as I have learned from years of research, advocacy, and community engagement, this is not an isolated incident. In fact, the child welfare system frequently jeopardizes the futures of its wards, with Black and other racially/ethnically minoritized youth bearing a disproportionate brunt of its failures (Johnson, 2021).

In this chapter, I confront this paradox head-on. I explore the foster care system's historical complexities and examine the lived experiences of the young people who, despite the odds, find ways to resist and challenge a system that often seems designed to oppress them. But before we delve into these narratives, let us first look back at the history of foster care to understand the roots of these contemporary failures.

THE FOUNDATIONS OF AMERICAN FOSTER CARE

Charles Loring Brace, a minister who founded the New York Children's Aid Society in 1853, is considered the father of the modern American foster care movement. He was concerned with the growing number of children residing on the streets of New York City, many of whom were recent immigrants facing language barriers, poverty, and the typical challenges of city life without familial support. Thus, in 1854, Brace initiated what later became known as the Orphan Train Movement (OTM)—an early iteration of the foster care system (Seita, 2018; Trammell, 2009).

The historical operation involved relocating these individuals from the congested urban areas of a major city to residences across different regions of the country, primarily in the Midwest, West, and South. Over the span of 75 years, from 1854 to 1929, this movement successfully resettled an estimated 200,000 individuals (Trammell, 2009). While the endeavor was initiated with benevolent motives, aiming to offer these individuals safety, security, and opportunities for a better life, it faced challenges. Due to the absence of legislation for safeguarding children and standardized protocols during that era, the program lacked stringent supervision. After the youth were placed with host families, there was minimal to no ongoing monitoring. This lack of post-placement support, combined with the reality that many host families underwent no prior vetting or assessments, resulted in some individuals being placed in suboptimal and occasionally exploitative environments.

A significant unintended consequence of the OTM was that some of the relocated children ended up as indentured servants. Tasked with arduous labor and domestic chores, they faced conditions not dissimilar to the hardships they endured in New York (Trammell, 2009). The OTM is only one pivotal moment in the history of child welfare reform in America. The case of Mary Ellen Wilson is another.

In 1874, Mary Ellen, a 10-year-old girl from New York City, was discovered abused, constrained, and malnourished. Her story accented the glaring absence of and need for a child protection system. In lieu of such a system, advocates on her behalf sought the formal intervention of the American Society for the Prevention of Cruelty to Animals. Her case catalyzed the development of the New York Society for the Prevention of Cruelty to Children in 1875, the first state child protection program (Jalongo, 2006). Since then, several significant legislative actions have been taken that shaped and defined America's foster care system (Myers, 2008; see Table 2.1).

Despite these reforms, many young people in foster care today face realities that fall short of the protective measures envisioned by these laws. The foster care system has, from its beginning, struggled with fulfilling its promise of safety and security—much like the Orphan Train Movement, which intended to remove children from the squalor of NY streets but often led them to uncertain futures and, for some, conditions mirroring the very streets they were meant to escape. Those early missteps reverberate for young people in care today.

How the Foster Care System Works

Figure 2.1 presents an adapted depiction of how the foster care system works. A young person may enter the system through a voluntary surrender by the caretaker or removal by the state due to issues such as neglect or abuse. Removal initiated by the state typically occurs in response to an allegation reported to the local child welfare agency, or when the police respond to a call. Additionally, a young person may enter the system if their primary caretaker is incapacitated due to death, incarceration, or hospitalization. When a substitute care setting, or placement, is deemed necessary, it must prioritize the least restrictive and most family-like environment suitable for the child's needs (Gross & Geiger, 2018).

Kinship care, which involves the young person staying with a relative, whether by blood, marriage, or other bonds, is the preferred placement for children due to its less restrictive nature and the maintenance of familial ties (Gross & Geiger, 2018). Nonrelative foster care, as the name suggests, involves a licensed foster parent or parents providing temporary out-of-home care for the young person. It is used when kinship care is unavailable.

Table 2.1. Overview of Significant Legislation Impacting Foster Care

Year	Legislation	Description
1935	Social Security Act (SSA)	Part of Franklin D. Roosevelt's New Deal, this act groundwork for federal financial support for state-run child welfare programs to assist dependent children.
1960	Flemming Rule	This administrative rule was named after U.S. Department of Health, Education and Welfare Secretary Arthur Fleming. It expanded the scope of the Aid to Families with Dependent Children-Foster Care (AFDC-FC) program, banning states from denying program benefits to families based on the "unsuitability" (e.g., children born out of wedlock) of their homes. The rule thus required that states provide support services and care to these families or place youth in foster care.
1961	Amendments to Title IV of Social Security Act	This amendment expanded the AFDC-FC program to include foster care payments. As a result, states were allowed to use federal funds to support foster families. Family preservation services were also encouraged to prevent the removal of children from their homes.
1974	Child Abuse Prevention and Treatment Act (CAPTA)	This act allocated federal funding to states for the prevention, identification, and treatment of child abuse and neglect.
1980	Adoption Assistance and Child Welfare Act	This act aimed to keep families together, ensure children were placed in the least restrictive, most family-like settings, and reduce extended stays in foster care.
1993	Family Preservation and Support Services Program Act	This act allocated federal funding to states for programs to keep families together, ensure children's safety, and reduce the necessity for foster care placements.
1997	Adoption and Safe Families Act (ASFA)	ASFA prioritized the safety and permanency of children in foster care and expedited the process for freeing children for adoption.
1999	Foster Care Independence Act (Chafee program)	This program established the John H. Chafee Foster Care Independence Program, offering states flexible funding to support youth transitioning from foster care to self-sufficiency.

(*continued*)

Table 2.1. *(continued)*

Year	Legislation	Description
2008	Fostering Connections to Success and Increasing Adoptions Act	This act bolstered provisions relating to the health and educational well-being of children in foster care, promoted permanent family bonds, and ensured sustained family connections.
2010	Child and Family Services Improvement and Innovation Act	This act extended funding for specific programs and allowed states added flexibility in devising innovative approaches to child welfare services delivery.
2018	Family First Prevention Services Act (FFPSA)	This act was designed to prevent at-risk children from entering foster care by offering more services to such families and stressed placing children in the most familial settings when removal was necessary.

Alternative placement possibilities encompass therapeutic foster homes, group homes, residential treatment centers, and monitored independent living. Therapeutic foster homes have specically trained foster parent(s) who care for youth with more complex behavioral, emotional, or mental health needs. Group homes—smaller-scale, 24-hour residential setups—distinguish themselves from larger institutions. Residential treatment centers are live-in healthcare facilities that, like therapeutic foster homes, provide intensive therapy for youth with serious behavioral, emotional, or mental health issues. New placement types were created for older youth in care (age 18+) following the Fostering Connections to Success and Increasing Adoptions Act that extended foster care. These include Supervised Independent Living Placements (SILPs), which present an alternative avenue wherein young individuals can cultivate greater autonomy under the oversight of an agency, although not on a 24-hour basis (Gross & Geiger, 2018).

During placement, a judge may periodically hold judicial hearings or reviews to ensure the child's safety. A case plan is often developed, detailing the services provided to the caretakers, the case goal (such as reunification), and the supports in place for the youth who has been removed from the home. Frequently, caretakers who have had a child removed are required to meet specific goals and conditions as stipulated in the case plan to regain custody (Gross & Geiger, 2018, p. 48).

While the primary goal is family preservation, and the state works diligently to address the issues that led to the removal of a young person from their home, alternative permanent placements are also sought in instances where reunification may not be possible. A young person may

Figure 2.1. Overview of Foster Care Process Adapted from Geiger & Gross (2019)

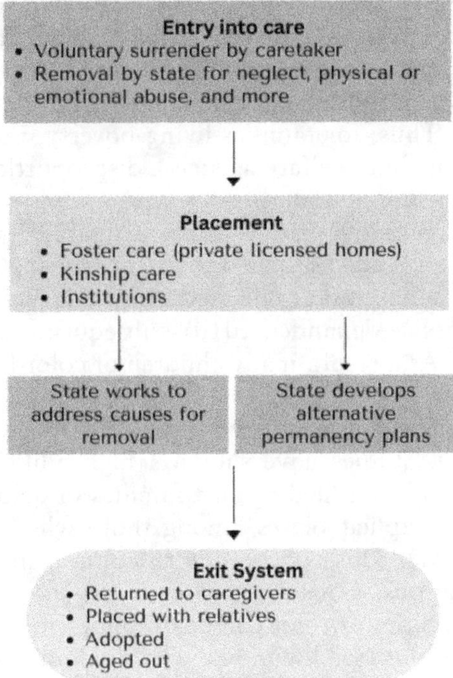

exit the system by being reunited with their caretaker, being adopted, entering a legal guardianship arrangement, or aging out if they reach their state's age limit without achieving one of these permanency arrangements (Gross & Geiger, 2018).

As young people often find themselves moving from one placement to another, they face disruptions in their education and emotional development. And as youths age out of the system, the support they receive during this transition is often minimal, making their passage to independence fraught with challenges. Additionally, maintaining biological family connections and securing permanent adoptive homes continue to be significant concerns.

Racialization of the Foster Care System

As the foster care system in the United States evolved over the years, so too did the racial composition of its youth. The system transitioned from primarily serving White children to one being overrepresented with Black and other racially minoritized youth by the mid-20th century

(Billingsley & Giovannoni, 1972; Pelton, 2010). This shift, in part, related to aftermath of World War II, which resulted in significant demographic changes, included the relocation of Black families from the rural South to urban communities in the North. Moreover, racial segregation and other economic impediments helped create concentrated areas of poverty. Thus, for families living poverty, they faced heightened scrutiny from child welfare agencies, disproportionately affecting racially minoritized communities.

The War on Drugs in the 1970s is also culpable. Its enforcement of rigid drug laws supposedly designed to discourage the production, distribution, and consumption of illicit led to mass incarceration of Black and Hispanic people (Alexander, 2010), subsequently disrupting many family structures. As a result, many children of color found themselves in foster care.

Other factors include biased reporting and investigations of child abuse and neglect. Studies have shown a higher likelihood of abuse and neglect reports being filed against families of color, influenced by both implicit and explicit biases among those who report suspected cases (Harris, 2021). This can be due to cultural misunderstandings and misinterpretations. Consider that practices that are deemed normative for communities of color can be misunderstood as neglectful or even abusive by White social workers, who predominate the field. This can result in an unwarranted and unnecessary child welfare intervention. That child welfare agencies have been found to investigate and remove children from families of color more frequently than their White counterparts under similar circumstances (Dettlaff & Boyd, 2020) is not at all surprising.

Leading scholars like Dorothy Roberts (2009) have raised questions about the function of the foster care system, suggesting that it functions more as a form of social control—a family separation rather than a protective system. This perspective is crucial in understanding how systemic racism and inequality have shaped the foster care system. Indeed, the racialization of the foster care system reflects deeply entrenched racial and economic inequities.

IN THEIR OWN WORDS: LIFE IN FOSTER CARE

Having provided some historical context about the foster care system, let's now turn to the stories of youth themselves. This section is dedicated to unpacking the systemic shortcomings through the lens of those who navigate its complexities daily. By centering the intersectionality of race, gender, and sexual orientation, I illuminate the diverse and compounding challenges students face. Through a synthesis of overarching themes drawn from multiple narratives and the in-depth personal accounts of an individual student, my intention is to provide a nuanced portrait of the lived realities within the foster care system. Now, meet NiQi.*

NiQi's Story

My doctoral student, Allante, was scheduled to interview NiQi—a sophomore in college identified as a Black woman—for our study. Unexpectedly, I had to step in due to a scheduling conflict. Logging onto Zoom early to preempt any technical glitches, I noticed NiQi already in the waiting room, her promptness a refreshing preview of her personality.

As I admitted her into the session, the screen lit up, presenting a young woman with brown eyes and dark Black hair. I greeted her: "Hello, I'm Dr. Johnson. Thank you for making time to speak with me today." Her smile was genuine. "It's no issue at all. I'm grateful someone cares to hear my story," she replied, her response easing the slight tension I felt—a common thread in interviews given the history of exploitation many participants faced.

We discussed the study's details and her rights as a participant, ensuring her informed consent before recording. Our conversation began with lighter questions about self-perception and external judgments, painting a picture of a person who was outgoing, sometimes absent-minded, yet lively. NiQi considered herself passionate, perhaps overly so, while others might see her activism for student voice in child welfare reform as overzealous.

With the backdrop of her preinterview questionnaire, I knew NiQi had identified as lesbian and had spent a significant portion of her life—11 years—in foster care. The reasons for her placement, however, were still a mystery.

Gradually, I guided the conversation to the core of her experience: "If you're comfortable, could you share why you entered foster care?" I've learned to anticipate a wide range of responses to this question, from heart-wrenching and traumatizing accounts to situations that called into question the necessity of foster care placement over less disruptive interventions. NiQi paused, her gaze steady. And with that, we ventured into her story:

---

* A pseudonym I am using to protect her identity. I use this practice for all students features.

> When I was 7, I was sexually assaulted by my mother's boyfriend . . . she didn't believe me. She actually kept seeing the man, even when the investigation was happening, and even after he had admitted to it, and was caught on tape doing it. We were immediately taken from her home. Again, this was probably about the 12th time it happened, if not even more. From that point on, it just seemed like nobody ever really wanted me. My sister ended up adopted. And I just kind of kept bouncing from home to home to home to home.

NiQi's response, while chilling, was unfortunately not unfamiliar to me. Prior to beginning this research, I had conducted training with my team to ensure we were all prepared to engage in trauma-informed research. With the guidance and expertise of our study's advisory board, we discussed the complexities of trauma and its potential impacts on the physical, psychological, emotional, and social well-being of youth we studied. We learned to navigate these stories with the utmost sensitivity, fostering an environment where participants could feel secure and validated. This training was now the framework within which I processed NiQi's story.

During one of her pauses, I leaned in, attempting to bridge the virtual space to offer some semblance of proximity and support: "Thank you for sharing that with me. I can't imagine how difficult that was for you." It was a delicate balance to strike—providing validation without overstepping into the realm of therapy. I maintained professionalism while extending her the choice to continue, change the subject, or end the interview, reaffirming her agency over her narrative. NiQi, seemingly recognizing the care and sensitivity with which I navigated our conversation, chose to proceed confidently. She resumed her story:

> My little sister was never taken from my mother's custody, which was . . . everybody finds to be really strange. My mother is actually currently . . . in prison for Munchhausen's by proxy, sex trafficking. . . . What is the other one? Sexual exploitation of minors, child pornography, all kinds of stuff like that. We were all separated, so I went to a foster home. [My sister] went to a foster home. She ended up getting adopted. My little sister stayed with my mother until she turned 18, and immediately left.

After she shared the circumstances that led to her placement in foster care, my curiosity naturally extended to her experiences within the system itself. I broached the subject with sensitivity, asking if she could elaborate on her time spent under state care, in response to which she directed our focus to one aspect in particular: her residential placements. "I've had so many [residential placement] changes. At least a hundred. I lost count. It was every 6 weeks for years. I was [at] a different home, [with a] different family, different school, different everything," she shared frankly.

The conversation about residential stability naturally segued into a discussion about the nature of NiQi's experiences with the case workers assigned to her during her time in foster care. She provided a rough estimate: "I had about 12, 13 in Florida. And then I had four in Georgia. And then I think I had five or six in Texas?" Her experiences ranged from indifferent to impactful. "In all honesty, I felt like they felt it was just a paycheck. They didn't really care," she noted. "I could tell them I wasn't being fed. I was severely underweight at the time, and they didn't care. I could tell them that they were drinking all the time, and we weren't getting fed, or we were being made to work to be fed. They didn't care."

NiQi paused for a second, before highlighting a rare exception. "I think I only had one social worker who actually seemed to care, and it was actually this Black lady. She was amazing." NiQi's voice raised a bit with excitement. "She helped me get on an IEP plan [Individualized Education Plan] for school so that they couldn't just kick me out of school because I was having emotional issues. She got me into tutoring. She got me into therapy. Any time I came to her with something, she was right there." This relationship was short lived though. "But when she got promoted, I ended up losing her, and I got somebody else that wasn't even anywhere near what she was."

NiQi's variable interactions with case workers was just one facet of her experiences in foster care. She shared that while in the system she also became a teen mother and was involved with the juvenile justice system. Each presented its own set of challenges, further complicating her already difficult journey.

Despite these challenges, however, NiQi was not deterred. In many ways, she spoke of her challenges not as defeats but as sources of strength and resilience. "In a kind of way, it's kind of helped me in the long run," she shared. "A lot of the things that I've experienced, a lot of the issues I've gone through have been the foundation for me to want more . . . to fight for more." Her voice was quite firm with conviction.

And it's not just herself who she fights for. Channeling her personal challenges into strength, NiQi is now a leader in her state and is an advocate for student voice in local state policy. "I think my own experience [has] given me the courage to stand up for others who might be in the same situation that I was in," she asserted.

Her eagerness to participate in this study was also part of her advocacy, she noted. "When I found about this study, I was like, 'Yeah, I want to do it,'" she shared. "I [never] want to see other kids to not feel like they don't have a chance . . . because that's how basically how I felt for a while . . . like there wasn't enough help or programs or even people who actually cared."

Despite her challenges, NiQi's present is a testament to her resilience: "I am an honor student now and in the running for the Jack Kent Cooke scholarship," she shared with excitement. She also shared she had been invited to apply for a graduate program at an Ivy league university, which she was very excited about. This opportunity, in many ways, was a symbolic victory over the challenges that once threatened to define her.

COMMON THREADS: THE CHALLENGES OF STABILITY, CARE, AND SAFETY

NiQi's story, though deeply personal, aligns with the experiences of others whom my team and I interviewed. In this section, I delve into some of these common threads that animate their time in foster care, revealing some of its systemic failures. Yet, in the face of these challenges, these young people derive motivation, even capital, to persist and advocate on behalf of themselves and generations to follow.

Residential Instability: The Revolving Door of Foster Care

When NiQi first mentioned experiencing "at least a hundred" residential placements during her years in foster care, changing locations approximately "every 6 weeks for years," I initially wondered if she was exaggerating. Such extreme instability seemed incongruent with the primary goal of foster care: to provide safe, stable, and nurturing temporary out-of-home care for young people facing abuse or neglect. However, it turns out this level of instability is not as implausible as it appears.

As I mentioned previously, participants completed a demographic survey questionnaire probing for basic background information, including the number of residential placements they experienced while in care. The responses were startling in their range, from none to "too many to recall." One participant even indicated 300 placements, though I'm hoping that was to illustrate just how outrageous their number of placements were, rather than the true number. Yet, as interviews progressed, the reality of most of these numbers became apparent. With responses like 6, 17, 23, 2, 12, 14, and more, it was clear that for many, foster care was a revolving door of homes and families—a far cry from the stability it promises.

This instability was not equitably distributed. Black and lesbian, gay, bisexual, trans, and queer (LGBTQ+) students in the study reported a comparatively higher number of placements compared to their peers. When asked to recall her residential placement changes in foster care, Mimi, a Black woman and 4-year college student, replied, ". . . around 50 or 60. That's including group homes and foster homes." Similarly, Doc Mills, a Black man in his fourth year of college, noted, "I never got adopted. I never was in a foster home. I've only done residentials or juveniles, or group homes. And, it was over 34." For context, Doc Mills was never placed with a foster family, what he is referring to as a "foster home." As a result of the child welfare system's inability to identify a more permanent placement for him, he frequently moved around various residential facilities. When he says "juveniles," he is referring to juvenile detention facilities—places that are all too common for Black boys and young men due to their heightened surveillance, punishment, and ultimately criminalization (Brooms & Clark, 2020; Johnson & Dizon, 2021; Noguera, 2003).

The higher level of residential instability that Black students in this research experienced is not unique. Findings corroborate broader trends suggesting that Black youth, on average, experience more frequent placement changes (Foster et al., 2011), which can have potentially negative consequences for their development, exacerbate feelings of rejection and unbelonging, and limit the formation of emotional ties with caregivers (Johnson, et al., 2020; Rubin et al., 2007). There are also educational consequences that deserve mention, but I will save those for the next chapter.

The experiences of LGBTQ+ youth are also noteworthy. Kris, a queer White nonbinary youth, shared, "I've lost count after about the 20th move. Many were because the families wouldn't accept my identity." Kris' experience exposes another layer of instability that is particularly salient for queer and gender nonconforming youth—not only do they navigate the systemic challenges of foster care, but they are also confronted with the need for acceptance of their sexual and gender identities in each new placement.

These inequities are exacerbated when one's intersecting identities come into play. Mia, a Black trans girl, described her foster care journey as "a search for a place to simply be myself. I faced racism in some homes and transphobia in others. Sometimes both."

What these stories illustrate is that residential instability in foster care is not just about moving from one placement to another. Such placements and one's experiences within them, are shaped by their identities. Youth with marginalized identities like Black and LGBTQ+

youth, and certainly those who exist at the intersection, are confronted with increased or even multiple marginalization.

Issues of Safety and (In)Security in Foster Care

Foster care purports to provide safe, stable, secure, and nurturing environments for young people who cannot be with their parents due to concerns with abuse, neglect, or other familial challenges. Moreover, it is designed to offer temporary care, with the primary goal often being reunification with family (Administration for Children and Families, n.d.; The Annie E. Casey Foundation, n.d.). However, the stories of NiQi and Ma'Khia Bryant, as discussed earlier in this chapter, illuminate a stark reality: the system often falls short of these goals, sometimes exacerbating the harm it seeks to prevent.

Like NiQi and Ma'Khia, the stories of participants in the research reveal a significant gap between the espoused intentions of the foster care system and the lived experiences of youth in it, particularly as it relates to challenges surrounding safety and security. These narratives not only highlight the system's failure to ensure physical well-being but also expose the emotional and psychological neglect that many youths in foster care endure.

Ella, an Asian woman currently in her third year of undergraduate studies, shared her journey through the foster care system, emphasizing the pervasive insecurity faced by so many others. She recalled her early experiences, saying, "My first experience was not great. . . . and [the staff at my group home] didn't take my mental health seriously. They didn't want me on antidepressants, even though I had severe PTSD, anxiety, and depression." Ella, a self-described "dedicated student," felt like "they didn't really care about what [she] was going through mentally," compounding feelings of precarity and insecurity.

Similar feelings and concerns were reflected in the stories of Amara, Jon, and Mary, who all shared a similar sentiment that they felt safer at "home," that being the place from which they were removed due to concerns of safety and neglect. At least in those settings, they shared, they knew how to navigate through the context. The abrupt removal and displacement to a new, unfamiliar context can be traumatic. It is even more traumatic when you're preoccupied with safety and whether your basic needs will be met. Amara, an Asian woman, shared that she was subjected to neglect and malnourishment in one of her many foster care placements, with a family who treated her very different than their biological kids. Such mistreatment exacerbated her feelings of disposability.

"Disposable" was a word Jon, a 1st-year Puerto Rican student, used when reflecting on his time in foster care. When probed about the source of this emotion, he shared a story about being "pushed out" of the home of his foster family of 12 years, which is a considerably long time to be in foster care without permanent placement, though not implausible. That Jon could be with and a part of a family so long and still be relocated abruptly without sufficient explanation, according to him, only illustrates the precarity that characterizes foster care placement for some. That precarity leaves youth feeling unsafe and insecure.

Mary, a White 1st-year college student remarked, "We deserve better, and our safety should always be the top priority." She went on to share her experience in a group home, which she characterized as "unsafe," noting, "Every night, I went to bed worried about if I was going to be attacked by someone. There were all these fights all the time, and girls [in the group home] would wait until you're slept to like get their lick back and attack you. It was one of the worse experiences in all of the time I spent in foster care. . . . just always worried." The hypervigilance that Mary describes was particularly salient among LGBTQ+ youth. Kris, who identified as nonbinary, and Mal, who is a Black pansexual man, both spoke candidly about the feeling of being at risk caused by discrimination and lack of acceptance of their identities. This ranged from a barrage of questions and sometimes outright hostility about who they are, to hypersexualization, which Kris said left them feeling "on alert," and thus not safe.

Relationship with Child Welfare Case Workers

The significance of the relationship and bond between young individuals in foster care and their child welfare case workers cannot be overstated. As aptly stated by Antle, Johnson, Barbee, and Sullivan (2009), this connection "is one of the most significant relationships an adolescent will experience" (p. 311). It's not just about the provision of services like crisis management, permanency planning, and transitional support. Rather, it represents a unique and profound opportunity for caseworkers to serve as exemplars, educators, and advocates, nurturing the development of healthy relationships among youth in foster care (Augsberger & Swenson, 2015). Unfortunately, such relationships are sometimes less than ideal.

Amara offered a very poignant reflection about her relationship with her caseworker when probed, noting, "My first case worker didn't really seem to care about us. I don't even know if she tried to get what we were going through honestly." This apparent lack of empathy and understanding fostered feelings of insecurity in someone who should otherwise be an advocate and support. Mark, a gay Latinx graduate student, shared similar sentiments. He highlighted how his case workers seemed to trivialize the challenges he faced. "They downplayed everything," Mark recounts. "Even when we faced problems with our foster parents, they justified it instead of helping us."

Both Amara and Mark's comments reflect a troubling dynamic where the very individuals tasked with safeguarding youth in care can (un)intentionally contribute to their feelings of inadequacy and neglect. This in essence is a systemic failure. Rodger, a Dominican and Puerto Rican undergraduate, had a journey marked by varying experiences with different caseworkers as well. To navigate these difficulties, Rodger admitted that he primarily relied on his guardian ad litem (GAL), a court-appointed advocate whose role is to represent the best interests of a child in legal proceedings, to "get the caseworkers to do what they needed to do." While his first caseworker was a source of inspiration and "motivated [him] to excel academically" and "aspire to a better life," his other one was dishonest to him and his birth mother about his status in care and other details about his placement. Rodger's story hints at the multifaceted nature of these relationships, where a single caseworker can wield tremendous influence, for better or worse.

In these stories, we see how important the role of child welfare case workers is in lives of youth in foster care. Beyond their administrative duties, they bear the responsibility of cultivating empathy, understanding, and advocacy.

NAVIGATING SYSTEMIC FAILURES WITH RESILIENCE

The stories shared in this chapter of the young people who I learned from illustrate some of the stark realities of the failures of the foster care system despite its espoused goals. For instance, the revolving door of residential placements that so many of these youths have endured is inexcusable. This challenge is particularly pronounced for Black and LGBTQ+ youths, who reported higher numbers of placement changes, underscoring the role that biases play in shaping students' experiences in the system. "I've lost count after about the 20th move. Many were because the families wouldn't accept my identity," Kris shared, highlighting the additional layer of instability faced by queer youth of color. The failure to offer consistent, safe, and nurturing environments to all young people in care is a glaring shortcoming.

Stories from students also suggest that the foster care system often falls short in its promise of safety and security. Ella's experience of having her mental health concerns dismissed by her case worker is a clear form of neglect that some experience in care by the folks who should otherwise be their zealous advocate. Moreover, Mary's account of the constant fear and hypervigilance she experienced because of physical threats illustrates how paramount safety issues within the system are.

Despite these systemic shortcomings, there are also stories of resilience, determination, and agency. Amara's declaration of independence captures this sentiment. "I feel like I'm . . . I'm, like, as independent as I need to be because I don't need anybody's help. Like, maybe I want their help, but I definitely don't need anybody's help," she asserted. Similarly, others have exhibited this same spirit of self-reliance, firmly believing that they can overcome challenges through their own efforts.

The desire for independence that some students expressed was not just a matter of preference but one of necessity as well, stemming in part from the precarious predicament they were placed as well as challenges associated with their identity. "Part of it is foster care, part of it is just overall being a Black person and the struggles we have to face . . . so we have to be independent," Mia shared.

When asked how they approached challenges, the resounding response was to face them directly. "I face it head on. I learned that [very] quickly. There isn't much room to not do so," Jon shared. To be sure, that youth feel like they have no other option but to face challenges directly is concerning, as challenges come with consequences. Still, Jon's approach and that of so many others is evidence, at least in part, of the grit that is nurtured out of their hardship.

Exemplifying the savviness in which some youths have developed to skillfully navigate unhelpful systems, Missy, a young Black woman, shared: "I never truly relied on my caseworkers. I couldn't be sure they were telling me the right things and sometimes it seemed like they just didn't want to be helpful. . . . I knew my guardian ad litem and attorney." Thus, at times when her caseworker was not supportive or difficult to work with, Missy used her GAL to ensure her voice was heard and that her rights were protected during court proceedings. Missy was not just a passive recipient of care but was agentic in shaping her reality and future.

CONCLUSION

In this chapter, we have covered a lot. From the historical foundations of the foster system to the lived realities of those who must navigate it, one thing is clear: despite its purported aims, it often falls short of its promise to provide safety, stability, and security. These system failures are most pronounced for Black and racially minoritized youth, as well as those from LGBTQ+ communities, exacerbating their vulnerabilities and challenges.

The paradox of a system designed to protect yet often harming those it serves forces us to confront an essential question: How can foster care be reformed to truly nurture the well-being of all children? Or can it? Systemic change requires that we move beyond addressing symptoms of systemic failures to root causes: racial biases, inadequate training for caseworkers, and the need for better support systems.

In the next chapter, we delve into how some youth, despite system failures, formulate and maintain college dreams. They activate often undervalued forms of capital, rely on a constellation of protective factors, and draw on hope to propel them forward to their goal of college, against the odds.

CHAPTER 3

"A Hope in the Unseen"

Navigating K–12 Education and Fostering College Dreams

In the early days of my doctoral studies, my graduate adviser gave me a copy of Ron Suskind's *A Hope in the Unseen* (1998) with a simple recommendation: "Read this; I think it will resonate with you." He was right; it resonated with me powerfully. At the time, I was deeply self-reflective about my own educational experiences as a young Black man (see Johnson, 2013), and those of others like me, who somehow successfully navigated seemingly insurmountable odds. I grew up on the West Side of Chicago, a drug- and violence-ridden community that exposed me to a litany of faced risks that could have easily derailed my educational journey. Yet there I was, a doctoral student at one of the top higher education graduate programs, defying the odds. Today, I am a tenured professor at USC who has written my first single-authored book, which you're reading.

A Hope in the Unseen is a powerful book that chronicles the story of Cedric Jennings, a young African American student navigating the challenging realities of inner-city Washington D.C., while striving to realize his dream of attending an Ivy League university. Cedric's story is one of determination, resilience, and the transformative power of education in overcoming adversity. Just as his journey was laden with obstacles, yet buoyed by hope, the experiences of many youths in foster care, particularly those whom my team and I interviewed, have similar contours. These young people often find themselves navigating educational turbulence, compounded by their experiences in foster care, some of which were shared in the previous chapter. However, like Cedric and myself, they possess a relentless drive and an unwavering hope—a hope often unseen by those around them.

This chapter aims to illuminate the formation and maintenance of college dreams among youth in foster care amid a backdrop of concerning challenges that would otherwise deter and alter their educational trajectories. Despite such challenges, they activate often undervalued forms of capital, rely on a constellation of protective factors, and harness hope to propel them forward to their goal of college, against the odds. Allow me to thematically share some of the challenges that shaped the K–12 education experiences of the students who I learned from.

K-12 EDUCATIONAL CHALLENGES

Residential and School Mobility and Its Consequences

As we explored in Chapter 1, foster care can often be akin to a revolving door of uncertainty for youth, particularly for those with minoritized identities, who disproportionately face frequent residential placement changes. These changes, though sometimes necessary, bring with them a number of educational consequences. Typically, a change in residence for a young person in foster care necessitates a corresponding school transfer, especially if their new home is outside their current school's district or if commuting to their current school becomes impractical.

The impact of these transitions on one's educational continuity is significant. Each new school a student attends often means acclimating to different teaching styles, curricula, and peer groups. Shanice, a 22-year-old Black woman who entered foster care at age 15 and reported changing high schools five times, described feeling perpetually out of sync:

> I was in high school when I got placed in foster care and you know that's such a pivotal time in one's journey. I knew I wanted to go to college, for sure, that was a given, but it's hard to prepare when you're pretty much constantly moving around. Every teacher was different. Every school was different . . . and I feel like every time I was kind of getting into a flow, you know . . . I would be moved again. So, it's hard to feel settled and I feel like kids need to be settled.

This perpetual state of starts and stops, particularly disruptive for those aiming for college, makes meeting academic benchmarks for college readiness a significant challenge.

These frequent moves also complicate the management of academic records. The transfer of essential educational documents and records often lags, leading to misplaced or delayed transcripts and, consequently, incorrect course or grade-level placements. Matt, a White 22-year-old 1st-year freshman who transferred schools three times in foster care, recalled a particularly frustrating experience:

> After one of my moves [school transfer], my transcripts took so long to arrive that the school made me retake classes I had already taken at my last school . . . and by the time they arrived I was so far in the school semester that they wouldn't let me change. So, I pretty much lost a year, and I was taking classes with students who were at a different grade level. It was a big setback for sure.

But the impact extends beyond academics. The social and emotional toll of repeatedly changing schools is significant. Building lasting relationships with peers and teachers becomes increasingly challenging, often leading to feelings of isolation and alienation. Amara, who experienced multiple school changes, shared her struggle with forming friendships and feelings of unbelonging:

> Every new school was like starting over again. I didn't know anyone, and it was hard to establish new friendships because everyone pretty much has their crew. So, at some point I just stopped trying. I completely disengaged. Even when some folks would be nice to me and try to include me in things, I just wouldn't engage. I would go to class, I would go home, I would go back to the . . . you know, whatever home I'm in and that's it. I would go to school and come home, I wouldn't speak to anybody. I would put my earbuds in, I would listen to music all day, I wouldn't pay attention in class, I would just be in my own world. I wouldn't speak to anybody, I would just . . . you know, do my own thing.

Amara's account, reflective of a broader trend identified in research (Johnson et al., 2020; Strayhorn, 2018), highlights the profound need for a sense of belonging in school environments. The absence of this belonging can lead to disengagement and antisocial behaviors, as students like Amara retreat into themselves when confronted with marginalization and alienation.

Moreover, the continuous need to adapt to new environments and the consequent feeling of disconnection can significantly impact a young person's sense of security and self-worth (Strayhorn, 2018). In the long term, this emotional exhaustion and disorientation due to constant change can cumulatively affect their overall well-being and academic success. Such instability risks not only their immediate educational outcomes but also their future prospects and mental health.

As is evident, the intersection of residential and school mobility can significantly impact the academic progress, social connection, and emotional health of youth in foster care. The narratives of these students underscore the importance of current legislative action requiring child welfare and education agencies to collaborate and improve educational stability and outcomes for youth. Notably, the Fostering Connections Act (FCA) mandates child welfare agencies to maintain a child in their school of origin unless a change is deemed in the child's best interest (FCA, 2008). Additionally, the Every Student Succeeds Act (ESSA) of 2015 introduced provisions ensuring that students with foster care experience stay in their school of origin post-placement change, unless a move is considered beneficial. It also stipulates that receiving schools must immediately enroll students lacking records and promptly request academic records from previous institutions. However, as illuminated by participants' experiences and corroborated by research (Clemons et al., 2017), a significant gap exists between these policy intentions and their real-world implementation, indicating a systemic failure to effectively address the educational needs of youth.

Intersecting Challenges of Bullying and Stigma

The narratives shared by youth also offer significant insights into their social experiences at school, highlighting their vulnerability to bullying and social stigma, not only from peers but from educators as well. This vulnerability is exacerbated when their multiply marginalized identities, such as race, gender, or sexual orientation, intersect. Stigma, in this context, refers to the disapproval of or discrimination against an individual based on perceived differences or characteristics, such as being in foster care (Goffman, 2009; Latalova et al., 2014). These compounded biases can critically undermine one's self-esteem, mental health, and overall schooling experiences (An, Lee, & Chung, 2020; Rose et al., 2019).

Amara, a Chinese bisexual woman formerly in foster care, reflected on her challenging school experiences:

> [Middle and high] school was tough. Being Asian, and being bisexual, it felt like there were so many reasons for people to pick on me. And being in foster care didn't help. I got a lot of bullying for anyone of those [identities], but especially for being Asian. It really got to me, and I guess I responded the only way I thought I could—I became pretty aggressive. That just led to a whole lot of trouble. I got suspended a lot, and it got so bad that I ended up in an alternative school.

Her experience with compounded, intersectional stigma (Berger, 2010) is not unique among youth who hold intersecting marginalized identities. Their stories often reflected a struggle against multiple layers of interpersonal and structural oppression, manifesting as bullying, subtle microaggressions, and structural stigma. For instance, some students recounted difficulties in participating in extracurricular activities due to their foster care status—such as unstable transportation, frequent residential changes, and administrative hurdles related to obtaining necessary permissions from foster care agencies—that often barred them from consistent participation in sports teams, clubs, or other school-related activities. These structural barriers deprived them of valuable experiences and skill development, further contributing to their sense of isolation and difference from their peers.

Rodger, a Puerto Rican and Dominican young man, also shared his experiences with peer bullying linked to his foster care status and ethnicity:

> Once people at school found out I was in foster care, they definitely treated me different. I heard things like 'my parents didn't love me' or 'I must have done something bad to end up in foster care.' But it wasn't just about being in the [foster care] system. There were stereotypes [kids would make about me being] Latino too. . . . [They] would say all types of [hurtful] stuff as if me being in foster care was related to my family background—like assuming there were problems at home typical of what they thought a Latino family was like.

The intersection of foster care status with other marginalized identities, like race in Rodger's case, can create a unique set of challenges. For example, internalizing negative stereotypes can significantly impact self-image and confidence, as experienced by Diamond, a multiracial 19-year-old woman who spent 5 years in foster care. She shared, "At some point you start believing the [negative] things people say about you. Like is something wrong with me? Is it my fault I'm in foster care?"

The stigma faced by these youths was not limited to interactions with peers. Many shared experiences with teachers who, sometimes (un)consciously, held biases against youth in foster care, also impacting their academic engagement and self-perception. Diamond recounted an incident from middle school that left a lasting impression on her:

> In class we [were] having group conversation about our future careers and aspirations. I shared I wanted to be a veterinarian because I just loved taking care of animals and my foster family at the time had two dogs that I always took care of. In front everyone, my teacher was pretty much like "maybe you should think about something more realistic based on your situation." Maybe she didn't mean it be hurtful in way it came [across] but it just seemed like she had [written] me off [because] I was in foster care.

> I always think about that experience [because] it just made me question myself and my goals for a long time.

Diamond's story offers a poignant example of how subtle, yet impactful, teacher biases can be. This incident not only undermined her educational and career aspirations but also reinforced a problematic narrative that her potential was circumscribed because of her foster care status. Such experiences can significantly dampen a student's enthusiasm for learning and their belief in their own abilities. It can also unfortunately prompt other students in the class to treat a student differently based on their foster care identity. That youth in foster care often confront lower expectations about their capabilities and potential is unfortunately uncommon (Smith, 2017).

Lack of Educational Resources and Advocacy

One particularly salient challenge youth spoke about was related to a lack of educational resources and advocacy. By educational resources, I mean enriching learning experiences and programs commonly available to other students, often accessible without the barriers of restrictions or bureaucratic red tape. These include activities such as summer programs, field trips, and after-school tutoring, as well as access to modern technology and reliable internet connectivity. These are not mere luxuries; they are crucial experiences and resources that significantly contribute to enhancing academic self-efficacy, shaping and forming positive dispositions toward college, and increasing readiness for college (Conley, 2007; Hossler & Gallagher, 1987).

Participation in extracurricular activities and enrichment programs, such as basketball, cheerleading, camp, or intensive summer academic programs, was often constrained for youth in foster care. These limitations arose from various factors. Frequent residential placement changes, described in an earlier section, made it difficult for youth to commit to long-term engagements. The instability in their living arrangements disrupted their ability to establish roots.

Moreover, activities that required travel for extended periods or involved financial costs frequently presented barriers as well. This is reflected in an experience recounted by a young White woman, Isabelle:

> I really wanted to be in this the summer science program . . . Ever since I was little, it was like this big dream for me. But with all the moving around [in foster care] and the expenses that came with the program, it just didn't work out. I remember feeling kind of left out, you know? It felt like I was

> losing a big chance to get ready for college, something that really mattered to me.

As reflected in Isabelle's experience, it's not just about participating in programs for the sake of participation. With a very clear goal of pursuing higher education, she recognized the importance of participating in an academic enrichment program like this as a strategy for increasing college readiness and competitiveness. Not being able to participate left her with a profound sense of exclusion and disappointment, underscoring how such restrictions can affect a young person's aspirations and self-esteem.

For students who fell behind academically in school, even attending things like after-school tutoring posed a challenge. Several students also recounted concerns about a lack of financial resources to participate in certain activities and programs that were designed to be enriching and supplementary to their learning experience but bore a cost.

Another common thread among these stories was the feeling of not having anyone advocating on behalf of their educational needs. Many expressed a sense of isolation in navigating these challenges, underscoring the pressing need for a more robust support system and advocates who can ensure that those in the foster system have access to the resources and opportunities required for their academic and personal growth.

Looming Fear of "Aging Out"

It used to be the case that most students aged out of the foster care system at 18, the legal age at which a state recognized them as independent and thus no longer eligible for support services. However, due to the Federal Fostering Connections to Success and Increasing Adoptions Act of 2008, which amended the Title IV-E foster care program, states now have the option of extending foster care to youth beyond age 18. Most recent data estimates suggest that 48 states, the District of Columbia, and American Samoa allow youth to extend support services beyond 18. Typically, youth who elect to extend foster care must meet specific requirements related to education and career goals. Access to information about such provisions for services, however, is not equitably distributed, fostering a looming fear of "aging out" among many who don't receive it.

One significant barrier to information is related to strained relationships with case workers, as discussed in the previous chapter. Students reflected on how their relationship with their caseworker often hinges on the quality of information they receive. Consider this quote from Missy:

> I realized there was just so much [she] didn't share with me. There are certain deadlines and stuff you got to meet and expectations if you want to continue getting support from the state and she didn't tell me about any of that. My birthday is November so I was like a year older than my classmates so I aged-out when I was in high school. I spent that entire year worried about what I was going to do. Thank God I ended up getting assigned [another case worker] because my old one got promoted, which is crazy to me because she was trash. But my new case worker was able to advocate for me and I eventually got extended. . . . I spent so much time that year though worried about my future when I should have been planning for school like everyone else was.

Missy's experience raises significant concerns, chief among them that case workers fall short in doing their most important job, which is to be zealous advocates on behalf of the youth they serve. The time and energy a youth expends worrying about their future and basic needs should be devoted to other meaningful activities and experiences, much like other youths have the privilege to do. This sentiment is further echoed by Doc Mills, who shared:

> I just remember feeling really anxious. At my school, we had a guidance counselor, Mr. Wright, who everyone worked with for college stuff. He pretty much answered everyone's questions. He connected you to college rep[resentatives] and he made sure we were all taking the examin[ations] we were supposed to. He would also check in on me [because] he knew I was in foster care, and I just remember feeling overwhelmed. Like how can I focus on that stuff when I don't even know if I'm going to be able to pay that shit? At that point, I'm like I'm responsible for myself so I have to make sure I'm good and can survive.

Doc Mills's experience draws a poignant distinction between the support available to students in traditional family settings and those in foster care. While some students are privileged to receive support from parents and family in addition to a dedicated guidance counselor like Mr. Wright, youth in foster care often do not share these privileges. Many, like Doc Mills, frequently feel like they are navigating life's challenges alone, with minimal support, intensifying feelings of vulnerability and uncertainty.

This struggle becomes even more pronounced when youth are in their junior and senior years of high school, a pivotal time in their educational journey, especially for those aspiring to attend college. During these years, students typically prepare for entrance exams, visit prospective schools, and work diligently on admission applications. However, for youth in foster care, the looming prospect of "aging out" of the foster care system casts a long shadow of doubt and anxiety over these important years.

FOSTERING AND SUSTAINING COLLEGE DREAMS: BARBIE'S STORY

Thus far, we have delved into a broad, though not exhaustive, set of challenges that shape the educational experiences of youth in foster care—challenges that, for some, would otherwise eclipse the very possibility of higher education. We have examined issues such as frequent school changes and the compounded stigma of being in foster care, recognizing how these factors can create considerable academic and personal challenges.

Yet, while these challenges are significant, they do not define the entirety of these young people's experiences or their potential. My intention in presenting them is not to confine youth to a singular narrative of hardship and pain, as Eve Tuck (2009) cautions against. Instead, it is to contextualize the systemic shortcomings that often work against them, setting the stage to highlight their resilience, resourcefulness, and unwavering ambition. How do they develop and sustain college dreams in the face of such challenges?

The story that follows will offer a deeper exploration of this phenomenon. It tells the story of Barbie who, like Cedric Jennings in "The Hope in the Unseen," embodies the remarkable capacity to turn obstacles into possibility. Her journey exemplifies how hope, in tandem with community cultural wealth and various protective factors, can ignite and sustain high educational aspirations, even amid significant challenges. Barbie's story not only illuminates the "how" behind these aspirations but also provides insights into the "why."

Allow me to elaborate first on what I mean by hope and community cultural wealth. More than optimism or a positive orientation toward the future, hope encompasses one's goal-directed thoughts, the identification of multiple routes to reaching those goals, and their capacity and motivation to use those pathways (Snyder et al., 2002). For instance, a student's actions are guided in part by their goal of going to college. Despite challenges to accomplishing that goal, such as a lack of exposure to the requisite curriculum or a lack guidance, the student adeptly identifies multiple routes to their goal and is motivated to use these pathways.

This notion of hope resonates strongly within the framework of Community Cultural Wealth (CCW) as outlined by Yosso (2005). CCW refers to the rich "array of knowledge, skills, abilities, and contacts possessed and utilized" by racially minoritized people to navigate and resist systemic challenges. Its elements—aspirational, familial, social, navigational, resistant, and linguistic capital—are not merely assets; they are inherently intertwined with a hopeful orientation toward the future. In other words, these elements collectively help foster a mindset that values persistence, resilience, and the overcoming of adversity.

Therefore, I argue that youth of color in foster care can and often do maintain high hopes for college, despite barriers, because they come from cultural communities where an orientation toward hope is highly valued. These communities instill the importance of identifying multiple paths and strategies to overcome obstacles. In Barbie's case, her journey to college is not just a story of personal ambition; it is also a narrative shaped by her CCW, which provided the scaffolding for her hopeful outlook.

In Barbie's story, we see how the elements of CCW—her family's emphasis on the value of education that contributed to her aspirational capital, the social capital garnered from her mentors, her own navigational skills, and resistance to inequitable structures—converge with her goal of attending college. These CCW elements bolster her capacity to envision multiple pathways to her goal and reinforce her agency in pursuing them, embodying the essence of Hope Theory.

"When Things Started to Click"

Meet Barbie, a 19-year-old Black lesbian student at West State University. She learned about our research through another student who participated in interviews with us and shared the recruitment flier with her. I am grateful to students who spread information about the study to others, as identifying participants could be quite challenging. Barbie reached out to me via email, and my doctoral student, Allante, scheduled time for us to meet.

Prior to our interview, Barbie completed a demographic questionnaire, so I had some context about her before we connected. She had spent 5 years in the foster care system and experienced two residential placements, which she described later as being "lucky," as so many of her peers had far more.

During our first interview, we covered significant ground—it was one of the longer interviews I conducted, as Barbie was very open and willing to share. Employing my life story interviewing techniques,

I always remembered to probe about specific details, whether about people, emotions associated with events, or themes to mark particularly transformative moments or periods. In this interview, after extensively discussing her experiences in foster care and reflecting on what it was like to be in the system, Barbie talked at length about a period in high school, somewhere between her freshman and sophomore year, when, as she put it, "things started to click." Her language indicated a significant shift in mindset and approach to life.

"What exactly clicked?" I wondered. I leaned in to guide the conversation, and Barbie eagerly shared her story. She explained that this was when she realized her autonomy in shaping her future, evidence of her agentic thinking. Frustration stemming from constant placement changes within the foster care system, coupled with a particularly negative experience with a caseworker who seemed "out to get her," motivated Barbie to take control of her life. This moment was where her resistant capital shone through. Her negative experiences in foster care, instead of deterring her, motivated her to take the reins of her life under control and formulate her own goals, no matter how lofty. That goal was to attend college and become an engineer.

Curious about what she meant by "out to get her," I, of course, probed: "What do you mean by that?" "She seemed to be trying to make my life difficult, always questioning my actions, making me feel like I was a burden," Barbie explained. "But I decided I couldn't let her or anyone else dictate my future." She drew here on her resistant capital.

This decision marked a "turning point" in Barbie's life (Rutter, 1996; Hasset al., 2014). She keenly understood that to realize the vision she set for her life, she had to take control of it. This vision, she noted, involved going to college:

> I've always wanted to go to college since as early as I can remember . . . at first like to be a doctor or lawyer like pretty much every other kid, but as I got older I really gravitated to math and science, which was crazy because I don't really remember being good at that stuff . . . especially because [I] was always moving around so much, but as I got older I knew I wanted to become an engineer.

Despite initial struggles in science and math, Barbie had always been a diligent student. She self-reported a 3.5 GPA from high school, which was quite remarkable given the instability in her personal life. Barbie recognized, like so many other youth in foster care (see Tobolowsky et al., 2019), that education was one potential ticket to a better life.

Her ability to maintain high educational aspirations in the face of very real challenges is what Yosso (2005) refers to as *aspirational capital*. Despite the persistent low expectations Barbie encountered from her caseworker and other adults while in foster care, she held on to messages about the value and importance of higher education she received from her biological family as a kid, one source of her aspirational capital: "I came from a family that valued going to college. Before everything with my family [referring to when she was placed in foster care], we always talked about school and going to college," she remarked. It is through her aspirational capital that she formulated goal-directed thoughts.

Her journey through high school demonstrated her navigational capital, which enabled pathway thinking. Barbie became a self-advocate, researching and seeking resources beyond what was readily available. "I knew I had to be my own guide. I couldn't just wait for things to happen," she said, outlining her proactive approach to overcoming barriers. This mindset was a direct application of pathway thinking from Hope Theory—identifying and pursuing various routes to achieve her goal.

For instance, like other students we interviewed, Barbie went above and beyond to research things, fact-check information given to her by caseworkers and school personnel, and proactively seek out resources:

> By this time, I was getting ready to [enter] into my sophomore year, and I felt like I was running out of time. And in my state we didn't even have extended foster care at that time . . . though we do now, so I just felt like I was running out of time, I guess.

The looming reality of aging out of foster care can be quite daunting, as we learned in the previous section. However, this urgency fueled her persistence, a blend of her agentic thinking and navigational capital.

However, it wasn't just her own internal resources and faculties that she leveraged. Several important relationships with adults emerged as instrumental—relationships and connections, forms of social capital, operated as protective factors as well.

Barbie recounted a story of meeting the program coordinator of a local nonprofit that supports young people experiencing basic needs insecurity. She found out about the organization from social media (Twitter) and reached out given the concerns she had about aging out. "Meeting Mr. Stagg was one of the best things that could have happen to me. He was supportive and connected me with so many resources I should have known about . . . but didn't."

Barbie talked at length about a couple of other supportive adults, including a teacher she often relied on for financial and emotional support and guidance. She described her teacher, Mrs. Jones, as "God sent."

The importance of these kinds of relationships for young people in foster care has been documented elsewhere (Hass &. Graydon, 2009; Neal, 2017), particularly for youth like Barbie who have struggled with trust given past experiences with adults.

These relationships were vital, especially as Barbie moved through high school and more seriously engaged in academic study. She talked about Mrs. Jones being a broker of social capital—connecting her to important resources and people:

> When I got to my junior year and it was time to really start thinking about college, [Mrs. Jones] made sure I could visit schools . . . and connected me with people [in her network] who she knew could help me.

Moreover, Barbie continued to leverage resistant capital to overcome obstacles and persist in her pursuit of higher education. She actively sought out scholarships, applied for grants, and took on part-time jobs to contribute to her education fund. Her determination and resourcefulness paid off when she was awarded a scholarship that would help cover her tuition costs. This moment of triumph underscored her deep commitment to her dream of becoming an engineer and attending college. Barbie's story serves as a powerful illustration of how hope can be a driving force in sustaining high educational aspirations and making progress toward actualizing those aspirations, even in the face of adversity.

CONCLUSION

In this chapter, we have delved into the challenges that shape the educational experiences of youth in foster care, challenges that, for many, would appear insurmountable. We explored the disruptive effects of residential and school mobility, the intersectional challenges of bullying and stigma, the lack of access to educational resources and advocacy, and the looming fear of aging out of the foster care system. Yet, as we have seen, these are not just stories of struggle; they are narratives rich with resilience and hope.

Barbie's story is particularly compelling, illustrating how some youth are able to activate their undervalued forms of capital, whether aspirational, resistant, or navigational, to chart a path toward their dreams. For instance, the aspirational capital inherent in her family's values about education and her navigational skills in maneuvering through the education system were instrumental in her journey.

In the following chapter, we delve deeper into understanding the college-going pathway for these resilient youths. We will explore the factors influencing their college choices, their transition into college life, and the realities they face as freshmen.

CHAPTER 4

Choosing College as a Matter of Belonging

As I met with Wendy, a young White girl, for our second virtual interview, her screen came alive with the vibrancy and earnestness that only a 1st-year college student could embody. As she sat in her residence hall room, I could see a bulletin board of sorts hanging behind her, adorned with photos of herself and others who I assumed were close friends and family, given their prominent display in her room. Our interview began with the usual formalities of consent, but swiftly delved into the heart of her journey from foster care to the college she now calls home.

"Choosing [my college] wasn't just about the academics," Wendy shared, her voice slightly raised with excitement. "It was about trying to find a place where I felt I could really belong, somewhere I could grow not just as a student but as a person who's been through a lot." Wendy's journey through foster care had been tumultuous, marked by numerous residential and school changes and compounded by lingering traumas from her experiences in the system.

Throughout our extensive two-hour conversation, Wendy unpacked the nuances of her decision-making process for college. She spoke of elements often overlooked by many—the presence of support services for students with foster care experience, financial aid tailored to her unique circumstances, and a campus culture that was both welcoming and inclusive. "You know, it's not just the college you choose; it's also about how that college chooses to support you," she reflected.

Her transition to college, as she recounted, was not without its challenges. Wendy described her initial days on campus as both exciting and daunting. "It was like going into a whole new world. I was on my own, but luckily, I didn't have to figure out everything on my own when I got here," she said. Her story, admittedly not emblematic of the journey that many college students formerly in foster care experience, is illustrative with insights about how college personnel might better support such students as they transition from a life often marked by instability to a college environment filled with both new opportunities and challenges.

In this chapter, I focus on Wendy's story to shed light on the factors that shaped her college choice. Through her eyes, we can understand better the paths some resilient young people tread in their pursuit of higher education. Next, I zoom out to capture broader themes that characterize the transition to college experience for the larger group of students I had the privilege of learning from.

COLLEGE CHOICE AS A MATTER OF BELONGING

The process of selecting a college, commonly known as college choice, is a multifaceted decision-making process that students navigate through predisposition, search, and choice stages (Hossler & Gallagher, 1987). Although Hossler and Gallagher's model is widely recognized for its clarity in outlining this process, its linear framework may not fully capture the experiences of highly mobile and post-traditional students (Iloh, 2019), such as adult learners or youth in foster care who may not enroll in college immediately after high school. Despite this, the model provides a valuable, parsimonious overview of the complex decision-making involved in college selection, offering a foundational framework from which to explore the nuances of this process for different student groups.

An often overlooked factor in the extensive literature on college choice is how the fundamental desire to belong shapes postsecondary enrollment decisions, particularly for groups who experience heightened vulnerability to marginalization, such as youth with foster care experience. Psychologists (Maslow, 1943) have argued that belonging is a basic human need that all people are motivated to satisfy in social contexts. I argue that sense of belonging—defined as the extent to which individuals feel accepted, valued, and seen as an important part of a community (Hausmann et al., 2007; Strayhorn, 2018)—can play a critical role in shaping students' perceptions of college, influencing their predispositions toward higher education, guiding their priorities during the search process, and ultimately affecting their assessment of fit with a potential institution (see Figure 4.1). Wendy's story exemplifies this sentiment best, illustrating how her desire for belonging influenced every stage of her college choice process.

Wendy's Predisposition Toward College

Predispositions toward college are the early attitudes and intentions that frame a student's view on higher education (Hossler & Gallagher,

Figure 4.1. The Relationship Between College Choice and Belonging

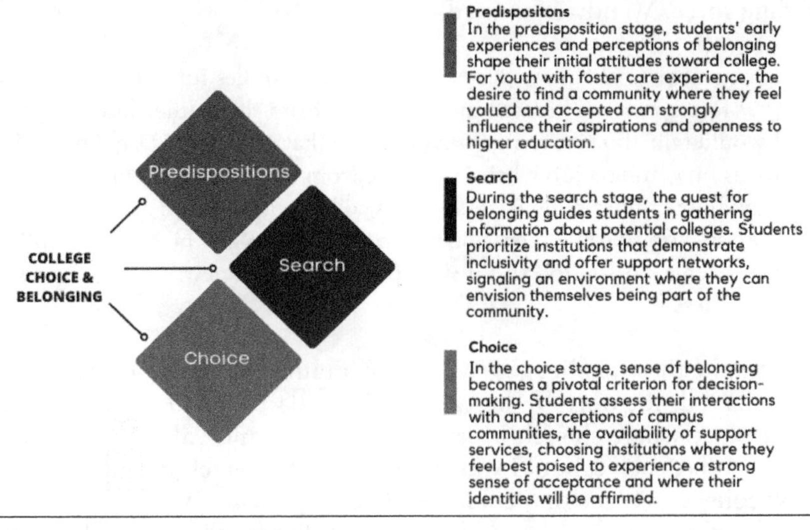

1987; Perna, 2006). For Wendy, this foundational stage was shaped significantly by her early family context and the values that her parents instilled in her. Recalling the profound impact of her biological parents on her aspirations for college, Wendy shared:

> College was pretty much a given. My [biological] parents both went to [State University]. So, I grew up valuing school and seeing it as something that I would do too. I think I wanted to be a veterinarian or something because I always loved animals. But I remember just having conversations with . . . them before they died about what I would be when I grew up. . . .

Wendy's strong value for education is unsurprising, given the significant role that parents' education levels play in fostering college aspirations for their children, as evidenced by decades of sociological and educational research (Sewell & Shah, 1968). One's value for education, along with their tastes, dispositions, and preferences, more generally constitute their cultural capital (Stanton-Salazar, 1997). Cultural capital is transmitted primarily by one's parents and other cultural brokers (Stanton-Salazar, 1997) like siblings and peers. Despite her journey through foster care, which involved frequent moves and chronic instability, Wendy retained this capital. Her residential placement changes meant confronting negative, low expectations and messaging about her abilities and education potential, factors that could have altered her favorable dispositions toward college education. Yet the positive messages and aspirations she harbored from her early years remained a guiding force. Wendy recounted:

> I remember . . . being with one of my foster families for about a year and [my foster parents] treated me differently from their other kids. Anytime I would talk about school or anything like that, they would say I needed to focus on getting a job when I graduate from high school. I remember they took [one of their biological kids] to a college visit and when I asked to go, they said no. It's like they didn't even want me to get the idea that college was even a possibility, so I just stopped asking. I knew I was going to go regardless.

Despite these challenges, Wendy maintained her aspirations for college, shaped not only by her academic goals but also by a desire to find a place where she felt accepted, respected, and valued. She stated: "Each home, each school I was placed in, I always felt like an outsider. I saw college as place that could finally be my own." Wendy's desire for belonging strongly influenced her positive dispositions toward college. She sought a campus where she was supported—a place she could call home, offering not just academic opportunities but also a welcoming and affirming community.

Wendy's path to college was marked by early aspirations formed under the shadow of loss and the resilience to hold on to her dreams amidst adversity. This illustrates a complex relationship between the predispositions toward college and the fundamental human need for belonging. To this end, predispositions come from a psychological need for belonging, which is derived from perceptions about what an ideal college would be like—one that offers acceptance and support.

Searching for Signs of Belonging

The journey through the college choice process extends into another phase where students actively seek out and evaluate potential schools—a phase that, as Perna (2006) observes, includes both the information students seek and the narratives institutions project about themselves. For Wendy, this search was less about the traditional markers of academic prestige and more about identifying a place where she could truly belong. Her approach underscores a nuanced understanding that belonging is both a personal journey and a response to institutional signals.

"Honestly, prestige was never my thing. It felt out of reach, and honestly, I was more focused on whether I could see myself there. Were there other students like me, and did the school have specific programs for us?" Wendy reflected. Her engagement in a state-run program designed to offer a bridge to youth in foster care to higher education highlighted the importance of college access and support initiatives. "They had ambassadors from the college who would connect with you, make you feel seen. That was huge for me," she said.

For Wendy, these programs were not just beneficial; they were essential indicators that a school might offer the sense of belonging she desired. These initiatives signaled that students with backgrounds like hers weren't just welcome but were a priority. "It was important for me to find a school invested in foster youth like me. I didn't really want to be alone. I want to be around other students like me," she shared.

Beyond the search for supportive programs, Wendy was acutely aware of the financial barriers that could impede her sense of belonging. The quest for financial security became an integral part of her search, aligning with scholars (Maslow, 1945; Strayhorn, 2018) who argue that financial stability is a precursor to belonging. It is hard to feel like you belong if you're constantly worried about how you're going to eat or where you're going to live. Thus, Wendy actively sought a place that would ensure her financial security: "I knew I had federal funds coming, but I also looked into scholarships and financial aid."

Her practical concerns extended to housing stability; a critical aspect often overlooked by her peers. "During my campus visit, I made sure to ask if I could stay in the dorm over summer breaks. Most students don't think about that, but for me, there was no 'home' to go back to. The dorm was my home," Wendy emphasized. This question was more than logistical; it was a litmus test for whether the institution could provide the continuous support and stability she needed to feel a sense of belonging.

Wendy's story about the search phase of her college choice process reveals a profound understanding that belonging is fostered not just through emotional and social support but also through institutional structures and resources that acknowledge and address the unique challenges faced by youth in foster care (Johnson, 2022). Her story is a testament to the multifaceted nature of belonging, highlighting the importance of institutional prioritization of students from diverse backgrounds, financial support mechanisms, and the creation of spaces where students can feel a continuous sense of security and community. Wendy concluded:

> I wanted to see myself reflected in the programs they offered. I guess it was about knowing I wouldn't just be surviving on campus, but that I could thrive there, I know that sounds kind of cliché but it's how it felt. It's how I still feel.

Choosing the Right Fit

At the heart of Wendy's college choice process was the profound sense of belonging she experienced during her campus visit—a pivotal moment that crystallized her final decision. "When I visited, I immediately connected with other foster youth like me. We have mentorship programs and advisors specifically for students like me. That was very affirming. Honestly, it just felt right," Wendy shared, her eyes lighting up at the memory. This sense of connection and support was not incidental; it was the result of a deliberate search for a community where she felt valued and understood. "You know, it's not just the college you choose; it's also about how that college chooses to support you. I felt like [this] college chose me as much as I chose it. It was the people, and just the overall vibe."

This stage of choosing the right fit goes beyond academic programs or campus amenities; it's deeply influenced by the emotional resonance and support structures that affirm students' identities and experiences. For Wendy and many other youths with foster care backgrounds, choosing a college is a quest for a campus that acknowledges their unique paths and integrates them into the community. "Meeting other foster youth and seeing the support in action made me realize that I wasn't going to be just another student navigating college alone. This was a place where my experiences as a foster youth were recognized," Wendy reflected.

The decision-making process, therefore, becomes a nuanced evaluation of how institutions not only meet academic and financial needs but also how they foster a sense of belonging. Wendy's experience underscores the importance of institutional efforts to reach out and support diverse student populations. "I felt like I mattered," she elaborated.

Choosing a college, especially for students from nontraditional backgrounds like foster care, is a significant life decision that extends beyond pragmatic considerations to encompass emotional and psychological needs. Wendy wanted to find a place where she could grow, learn, and thrive. Her early exposure and perspectives about the college environment signaled to her that she could indeed do that at her school of choice.

All in all, Wendy's narrative reveals the critical role of belonging in the college choice process, particularly for youth in foster care. Her story is a testament to the impact of institutional support systems and community engagement on students' decisions, offering important insights into how colleges and universities can create environments that are inclusive and identity affirming.

TRANSITIONING TO COLLEGE: NAVIGATING NEW BEGINNINGS

Transitioning to college represents a significant milestone for any student; however, for those in foster care, like Wendy, this transition is marked by distinctive challenges and opportunities for growth. In this section, we will explore the complexities of this critical juncture, exploring how some youth successfully navigate their entry into higher education. The discussion will highlight not only the resilience these students exhibit in the face of unique adversities but also the support systems that underpin their experience. By examining Wendy's story alongside broader themes from other students in this research, I will illuminate the commonalities and diversities in their experiences, providing a comprehensive picture of their transition to college and the factors that help support them.

Building a Supportive Community Through Campus Involvement

For students like Wendy, the transition to higher education is often fraught with unique challenges; yet it's also ripe with opportunity. Campus support programs (CSPs) designed for youth with foster care experience are important for their successful transition and belonging. Although they vary in size and scope (Geiger et al., 2016), they generally are designed to provide a range of academic, social, emotional, psychological, and financial support for students with foster care experience (Dworsky & Pérez, 2010), laying a foundation for their academic and personal growth. While the evidence base for CSPs is limited (Geiger & Beltran, 2017; Johnson, 2021), generally it suggests that students on average benefit from participation. Yet their efficacy varies widely, particularly when addressing the nuanced needs of students of color and those who identify as LGBTQ+.

Wendy's experience highlights the immediate impact such programs can make:

> I was overwhelmed when I first got to campus. The [CSP] became my go-to place. They helped me with enrollment, explained financial aid in a way I could understand, and introduced me to other foster youth on campus. It was comforting to know I had a place where folks [understood] me.

Wendy's initial engagement with a CSP underscores the critical support these programs can provide.

However, the experiences of other students, like Alex, offer insight into some of the nuanced challenges that arise when CSPs lack racial diversity or cultural competency:

> It offered workshops on everything from study skills to managing college life. It was [through that program] that I discovered scholarships specifically for foster youth and got connected to other programs and stuff. However, there wasn't a lot of [racial] diversity. [The program] was good in terms of getting me acclimated to [the university] but I felt disconnected sometimes. I was . . . the only Black student for a while and [the program staff member] didn't really know how to support me when it came to certain stuff. . . . I eventually got involved with the Black Student Union and that's where I really found my people.

Alex's sense of racial isolation within the CSP and the staff's inadequate racial literacy highlight a significant gap in support for Black students, driving them to seek community in spaces outside of the CSP like the Black Student Union.

Similarly, Maria's experience with mental health initiatives underscores the need for culturally and intersectionally competent support systems. "Joining the campus [LGBTQ+] alliance and finding a therapist who understood my [cultural] background [was important]," Maria reflects. Her journey to finding a community within the campus LGBTQ+ alliance and finding a culturally aware therapist speaks to the piecemeal approach students often must take to find supportive spaces that affirm all aspects of their identity.

Jordan's story further illustrates this point:

> As a creative, I needed a place to express myself, but also as a gay man, because those aren't really separate things for me. I saw [students in the organization] performing at the union one day and asked how I could join. Just having a space to express myself and just connect with other students who were like me helped, I would say.

Jordan's search for a space that embraced and affirmed both his creative and LGBTQ+ identities led him to a writing club that offered a sense of belonging and acceptance not fully provided by the CSP. This highlights the critical role of student-led organizations and clubs in providing nuanced support and community for students navigating multiple marginalized identities.

Taylor's involvement in the debate team not only provided a platform for personal growth and advocacy but also a community where he could navigate his identity and experiences as a young person with involvement in the foster care system. "Being part of the debate team taught me to articulate my thoughts clearly and advocate for myself and others with similar backgrounds," Taylor shared. This underscores the multifaceted nature of support necessary for the diverse student population within CSPs.

These narratives illuminate the critical importance of CSPs while also highlighting the limitations in fully supporting students with intersecting marginalized identities. The experiences of Alex, Maria, Jordan, and Taylor underscore the necessity for colleges and universities to adopt a more intersectional approach in their support services, recognizing that students often navigate their college journey through a complex interplay of identities. Institutions must expand and diversify their support initiatives, ensuring that all students, regardless of their racial, ethnic, or sexual identities, experience a community that affirms and supports their entire being. This not only aids in their immediate transition but also contributes to their long-term success and well-being, reinforcing the imperative for systemic changes within higher education to accommodate and celebrate the diversity of student experiences and identities.

Leveraging Institutional Agents

Beyond the foundational communities formed through campus involvement, students with foster care experience crucially leverage relationships with institutional agents (Stanton-Salazar, 1997)—faculty, staff, advisors, and mentors—who transmit their social capital. Indeed, these agents facilitate the activation of resources, guidance, and support mechanisms, playing an indispensable role in the education experiences of youth.

For students with foster care experience, the transition to college is marked by operate as important institutional agents, activating the students' social capital by connecting them with academic support services and supporting their transition into the college community. Wendy's narrative exemplifies this:

> I was struggling with feeling like I belonged in my major until Dr. Allen reached out me. . . . [She] really went above and beyond . . . not just [providing] academic advice; she connected me with alumni and other professionals in the field, and really opened doors I didn't know existed. She was a game-changer for me.

Stanton-Salazar emphasizes the role of mentorship in enhancing the social capital of marginalized students. Academic advisors and mentors, by understanding the unique backgrounds of youth with foster care experiences, tailor their guidance to address both academic and personal growth challenges. Alex shares how an academic advisor became a mentor and advocate: "Mrs. Carter went beyond advising; she understood the hurdles I faced as a foster care alum. She connected me with internships and on-campus jobs, empowering me to build my professional network early on." Alex's experience with Mrs. Carter illustrates how targeted mentorship can fortify a student's network of support, making academic and social transitions less daunting and more attainable.

The complex bureaucracies of higher education institutions often pose significant barriers to students with foster care experience. Institutional agents demystify these systems, guiding students through financial, administrative, and academic mazes. Maria's interaction with Ms. Rodriguez in the financial aid office underscores how informed, empathetic guidance from institutional agents can illuminate pathways to essential resources, reducing bureaucratic impediments to mere hurdles: "Ms. Rodriguez in financial aid was a lifesaver. She helped me navigate grants and scholarships specific to [students with foster care experience], making college financially feasible for me."

The academic disruptions common in the foster care experience can leave students feeling academically underprepared. Here, institutional agents offer tailored academic support. Jordan's relationship with a writing center tutor exemplifies this support: "Tom at the writing center didn't just help me with papers; he taught me how to express my ideas more clearly, boosting my confidence in my writing and my voice." Jordan's engagement with a writing center tutor, Tom, showcases how academic support, when aligned with the student's individual needs, can transform perceived academic weaknesses into areas of growth and confidence.

Institutional agents also play a crucial role in advocating for the inclusion and support of students within the broader campus community. Taylor's experience on the debate team, facilitated by Coach Hernandez, highlights how advocacy by institutional agents can foster a sense of belonging and community, crucial for the well-being and success of students from non-traditional backgrounds: "He wasn't just my coach, he was like an advocate. He ensured the team was a space where I could excel, pushing me to use my experiences as strengths."

These stories from students suggest that institutional agents are not merely supportive figures but are crucial actors in the activation and enhancement of social capital for young people with foster care experience. By bridging the gap between students and institutional resources, advocating for their inclusion, and addressing the unique challenges they face, these agents facilitate a smoother transition to college life, enabling students to adjust and ultimately thrive in college.

The Impact of Financial Stability on College Transition

Financial stability is very important to the college transition experience of students from foster care. This stability is not merely about alleviating financial burdens; it's fundamentally about empowering students to fully immerse in and maximize their college experience.

Reflecting on the impact of financial support, Wendy shares, "Having a scholarship and a safe place to call home, even during breaks, lifted so much weight off my shoulders. It wasn't just financial aid but a peace of mind." Wendy's experience underscores how financial security can transform the college experience, allowing students to focus on their learning and development.

Carlos, an environmental science major, echoes the significant influence of financial stability: "Securing a scholarship meant for us was life changing. It went beyond just covering my tuition. . . . I didn't have to worry about my next meal or where I'd sleep. It allowed me to focus on what really matters—my studies and future."

The importance of reliable housing is particularly significant, as Emma highlights:

> One of my biggest worries was always about where I'd spend the holidays or summer breaks. The university's commitment to year-round housing for students like me made this campus feel like home, removing a constant source of anxiety and letting me concentrate on my studies.

Zoe's reflection on her college journey illustrates the broader impact of financial stability: "Being financially secure opened doors to opportunities I never imagined were possible for me—joining clubs, volunteering, and studying abroad. These experiences made my college years better for sure, contributing significantly to my personal and professional growth."

These personal stories vividly illustrate that financial stability helps enable students to thrive—academically, socially, and personally. Scholarships, stable housing, and comprehensive financial aid are not just beneficial; they are essential for creating a supportive ecosystem that allows students with foster care experience to pursue their college dreams without the looming shadow or burden of financial insecurity.

CONCLUSION

The stories shared in this chapter, particularly through Wendy's journey from foster care to college, illuminate the complex challenges and triumphs faced by youth as they transition to higher education. These stories underscore a critical truth: the path to college for youth with foster care experience is not merely an academic endeavor but a deeply personal journey for belonging, support, and stability.

Belonging emerges as a central theme, a fundamental human need that significantly influences college choice and transition for these students. Wendy's story, alongside those of her peers, highlights the importance of finding a community where they can feel understood, valued, and accepted. Institutions that *proactively* create welcoming environments and foster a sense of belonging not only ease the transition for these students but also lay the groundwork for their continued success.

The indispensability of institutional support is further amplified in the stories of how students navigate their academic and social experiences with the help of institutional agents. Such agents include faculty, staff, advisors, and mentors who mobilize resources, offer guidance, and advocate on behalf of these students. This support system is vital for enabling students to demystify the complexities of college life, from academic planning to navigating financial aid.

Financial stability is underscored as another important factor, empowering students with foster care exerience to immerse themselves in their college experience without the looming worry of financial strain. Scholarships, secure housing, and comprehensive financial aid are not mere aids; they are necessities that allow students to concentrate on their academic pursuits and personal development, thereby facilitating a pathway to success.

In reflecting on the stories and insights shared in this chapter, it is clear that the journey to and through college for students with foster care experience is imbued with opportunities for resilience, growth, and triumph. These stories are not only a testament to the incredible resilience and potential of these students but also a call to action for college and university leaders. There is a clear imperative to continue enhancing and diversifying support mechanisms, particularly by leveraging institutional agents, to meet the unique needs of students with foster care experience comprehensively.

As we turn the page to the next chapter, the focus shifts to the critical aspects of retention and persistence. We will explore the strategies students employ to navigate their ongoing college experience, surmount challenges, and stride toward graduation and beyond.

CHAPTER 5

"Bridges" to Postsecondary Retention, Persistence, and Success

While a sizable number of youth with foster care experience hold high educational aspirations, the reality is that very few go from being hopeful applicants to enrolled college students. For those who do, an even smaller number make it across the stage for graduation. The roughly 8–10% who do is a sobering reminder of the considerable barriers these young people face, significantly reducing their odds of academic success. Over the past decade or so, scholars have nearly exclusively focused on the myriad factors contributing to this staggeringly low completion rate, noting frequent bouts of housing and food insecurity, lack of academic preparation and college readiness, and the absence of familial support, among many other factors.

What is less known and examined, amid the prevailing narratives of challenges, is the underlying spirit and the constellation of factors that enable the success of the 8–10% who graduate despite persistent and systemic institutional shortcomings. This group is replete with valuable insights into their own pathways to success, beyond mere enrollment and the initial transition to college, as access is merely the starting point. (Indeed, the absence of requisite supports to ensure and facilitate success beyond this critical juncture amounts to institutional negligence.) The stories of this resilient minority are filled with instructive insights, offering a roadmap on how we can better support and foster their success and thriving.

In this chapter, the focus shifts from the extensively researched barriers to the less-researched "bridges"—emphasizing not the obstacles these students face, but rather the forces that propel them forward. By delving into the success stories of this resilient group, I offer insight into some of the critical factors and support structures that facilitate academic success for youth with foster care experience. Like in previous chapters, I zoom in on a focal student, Dylan, to take a more in-depth look at individual experiences. And I zoom out to illuminate broader themes that resonate across the cohort of students from whom I was privileged to learn.

DYLAN'S STORY

As my research team and I were carrying out this research, the world was hit by a global pandemic. As a result, thousands of colleges and universities closed the doors to their campuses. This sudden shift to remote learning was a drastic measure to curb the virus's spread among students, faculty, and staff. However, an often-overlooked reality came to the forefront during this crisis: many young people with foster care experience, for whom college campuses provided not just an education but a stable living environment, suddenly found themselves without a "home" to return to. This oversight by higher education leaders highlighted a significant gap in the support system for some students, as campuses were not just academic refuges but also their primary source of shelter, food, and psychological support—essential elements for their learning, development, and overall success in college (Maslow, 1943; Strayhorn, 2018).

Among those displaced was Dylan, a young White man who, after entering foster care at 16 and navigating through a series of group homes, found a semblance of stability with his biological aunt. Despite some interpersonal challenges with his cousins, whom he lived with, Dylan described his housing arrangement as a temporary solution until he was able to get to college, which had always been his goal. "I just did what I needed to do . . . so that [my aunt] didn't send me back [to the group home]. I just kept reminding myself that it was temporary, and I just needed to hold out until . . . college," he shared.

And he did. Dylan held out, causing as little commotion as possible with his family, until it was time for him to enroll at Liberty University (a pseudonym). With funding from federal and state financial aid, specifically an Educational Training Voucher (ETV)—a program made possible through the Chafee Foster Care Independence Act—he enrolled, with not nearly as much stress or concern about meeting his basic needs as he had anticipated. Indeed, he embarked on his college journey with a sense of liberation and independence, finally. However, the COVID-19 pandemic abruptly halted his newfound independence, just a year and half into his college studies.

When Liberty University closed in Spring 2020 after his spring break, Dylan faced a familiar and daunting challenge: displacement. "I had been working so hard to feel independent and [feel] some sense of stability but all of that just went out of the window. I literally didn't have anywhere to go . . . but I had to leave my [residence hall]." While trying to maintain his commitment to school, particularly as a biology major, with aspirations of pursuing medical school in the future, Dylan found himself fighting to secure his basic needs—shelter, food, and a sense of safety, affordances so many of his peers didn't have to think about. "Everybody I knew went back home . . . [but] school was my home."

Forced to leave his residence hall, Dylan found himself in a precarious position:

> I spent the first couple of months couch surfing until I was able to figure things out. My friend Brian (a pseudonym) let me stay with him for a while. . . . I also stayed with Keith [my college roommate] for a while. They are like family to me though.

Couch surfing is in fact a form of homelessness, finally recognized in the 2011 revision of the McKinney-Vento Homelessness Act, that young people with foster care experience face increased risk of exposure to, particularly during the pandemic. The obviously transient nature of couch surfing, combined with the demands of remote learning, placed an enormous strain on Dylan's mental and academic well-being. "I honestly don't know how I got through that time . . . it was such a dark time, but I figured it out like I've always had to do."

Dylan did figure it out. To be sure, that he was placed in this predicament and forced to have "figure it out" in fact reflects a systemic failure and glaring institutional oversight. One clearly important factor, however, was the social and instrumental support provided by his "chosen family." In each interview, I probed students about their conception of family. For Dylan it was simple:

> It's the people who support you, have your back no matter what . . . not just the people you share blood with. I do have some good relationships with [my biological family] but it's my other family [nonrelatives] who support me the most.

Dylan's notion of family aligns with how scholars have conceptualized chosen family, referring to family that is not necessarily blood-related but formed through nonbiological kinship—a concept that was popularized by the LGBTQ+ community (Hull & Ortyl, 2019).

Brian and Keith, whom Dylan stayed with when his campus closed, were part of that chosen family. He noted:

> They were like the first two people I really connected with for real when I got to [Liberty]. I met Brian from class and Keith and I are roommates.

> Both are my brothers now. They knew I didn't really have family like that. . . . I shared with them [my foster care experience] at some point and [they] have been looking out for me ever since . . . even their parents embraced me. They are my family now.

And like family, Brian and Keith stepped in where systems had failed, providing not just emotional support but material support, from offering temporary living spaces to sharing meals.

Dylan also proactively tapped into his limited relationships on campus with staff, from the staff at the school's food pantry to the program director of his campus support program (CSP) for youth with foster care experience. Each of them acted as institutional agents, going above and beyond to support and connect him to critical resources. He shared:

> I didn't really participate much in [our CSP]. I definitely went more when I first got to [Liberty] but after a while I just stopped. But I did develop . . . I would say, a pretty good relationship with [the director] so I contacted her immediately and she was able to get me connected eventually to this program that helped me get my own place that summer.

Dylan was not well connected on campus. In fact, he admitted that he wished he had been more connected, as it might have helped when he found himself in need. Still, he displayed resourcefulness, proactively reaching out to leverage the few connections he did have. Fortunately, these relationships were an anchor during a difficult time. He shared, "I learned so much from that experience . . . just about myself and what I need to do differently moving forward, I would say. . . . I've definitely got more involved on campus since then."

Technology was also important in Dylan's persistence, helping to mitigate feelings of loneliness and isolation. Dylan and his classmates created online study groups and celebrated milestones virtually, maintaining a sense of connection amid the pandemic. Despite the virtual community, Dylan acknowledged the fatigue that eventually resulted from prolonged online interactions: "[My classmates] created Zoom study groups. We celebrated birthdays and other stuff online. It was good to stay connected but eventually were all Zoomed out," he noted. He, like so many students, yearned for physical, in-person connections that had been abruptly severed by the pandemic. Yet in these digital spaces he found reprieve, albeit temporary, from his current reality, while also maintaining some sense of belonging within the academic community. "It was like we were all in this together, trying to make the best out of a really tough situation," Dylan reflected.

This glimpse into Dylan's story and experience during a global crisis highlights his resilience and some protective factors that enabled him to continue. By leaning on his chosen family, leveraging relationships with institutional staff, and utilizing technology, he was able to overcome residential displacement and basic needs insecurity. His story offers some insight into the strength that is often required of youth in care to navigate our education system, while also shedding light on its shortcomings. In the following section, I highlight themes that resonated across the broader cohort of students related to how they navigate and overcome such shortcomings to persist toward their goal of degree completion.

Racial and Foster Care Identity Empowerment

Among the stories of Black students in the study, the saliency and intersection of their racial and foster care identities operated as a significant source of academic motivation and resilience. This theme aligns with identity-based motivational theories that assert that how people perceive themselves can have important consequences for their behaviors (Destin & Williams, 2020).

Black students were very aware of their racial identities and the relationship between those identities and their foster care history. Doc Mills, a Black man we heard from in an earlier chapter, shared:

> Everyone . . . knows that Black kids don't have the best luck in foster care. . . . It's just a given [that] you're likely not going to get adopted unless for some reason somebody in your family takes you [in], but otherwise, you're more than likely going to age out.

After further probing about how he arrived at this conclusion, he explained, "I didn't read anything, I just paid attention . . . and paid attention to how they [referring to staff in the foster care system] treat us. . . . [Black youth] don't have the same experience." Missy, a Black woman, affirmed Doc Mill's sentiment about differential treatment, noting, "That's why I advocated for myself. Case workers don't treat Black kids the same. That shit isn't fair but it's just the reality, I guess."

Both Doc Mills and Missy's comments demonstrate a keen racial consciousness that shapes their understanding of their social positioning within the foster care system and in society more generally. This awareness, however, acted as a catalyst for resistance and success, rather than discouragement. Missy alludes to her self-advocacy (we learned about other ways she did this in an earlier chapter), and she carried this proactive stance into her college life as well:

> When you look like me, people don't really have many expectations for you. That's part of the reason why I wanted to go to college. . . . I wanted to prove folks wrong. I think the more of us who do that, we can change the narrative.

For Missy, awareness of her social positioning at the intersection of her identities motivated her to go to school, in part, to resist stereotypes placed on her and youth like her.

To be sure, Missy, Doc Mills, NiQi, and others expressed pride in their identities as Black youth with foster care experience. This sentiment was evident in their stories. NiQi commented:

> I have gone through it all, but I know who I am . . . and whose I am. I used to feel bad for myself like why me, but everything happens for a reason. I embrace who I am and the good, the bad, and the ugly . . . when people ask me [about being in foster care], I don't lie about it. I tell the truth. It's shaped who I am, and I'm proud of that. There aren't a lot of Black foster kids in college, but I am.

NiQi's statement captures a sentiment shared among other Black students: their identities, while complex and filled with their own challenges, are integral to their sense of self, pride, and drive to succeed academically.

Contextual, environmental factors on campus also shaped their sense of self and identity (Destin & Williams, 2020). Black students struggled to be fully affirmed at the intersection of their identities both as Black youth and as youth in foster care. While involvement in the Black cultural center attended to their racial/ethnic identity, it did not engage with their foster identity. The reverse was true for student clubs and campus programs targeted at foster care identity. This prompted and inspired one student, Briana, to develop her own student club organization, specifically for Black students with foster care experience:

> I saw an opportunity and developed my own space. There were enough of us on campus, but there wasn't really a space for us. So, I talked with a few people first to see if they would be interested, and they were. My organization has been around only a semester, but it's growing.

Taken together, the stories from Black students in the study offer some insight into the ways in which their racial and foster care identities coalesce to shape their academic endeavors. Said differently, students' awareness of and pride in their identity positively motivated them to do well academically, resisting low expectations and negative stereotypes placed on them. And in the absence of affirming spaces that attended to their intersectional identities, they exercised agency to create such spaces for themselves.

Chosen Family

Dylan's story offers a cursory entry point for understanding how one's agency to self-author conceptions of family enables one's academic retention, persistence, and success. This concept extends beyond Dylan, though, resonating deeply with other students in the study who also developed and sustained nonbiological kinship networks. These networks served as sources of support, understanding, community, and belonging.

The formation of chosen families was not restricted to the campus community but rather encompassed a diverse and wide network of peers, mentors, social workers, and other community members whose love, encouragement, and material forms of support transcended other relationships in students' lives, resulting in their special designation as family. In all interviews, I probed students about their conception of family, asking them to define it. Responses often included definitions like "it is what you make it," and "people who got your back no matter what," and "relationships that are unconditional." For some students, however, this question was a source of pain, as it prompted frustration with their placement in foster care and strained relationships with biological family. For instance, one student, Mark, a gay Latinx man, offered the following reflection:

> When I came out to my [biological] family, they put me out [of the house], and I was homeless for a while. That's part of the reason why I was in foster care in the first place . . . and when I think about that, it just pisses me off because real family doesn't do that to their own.

Mark's experience is not an outlier, as it resonates with literature on the importance of chosen family more broadly for members of the LGBTQ+ community who are too often ostracized and alienated from their biological family due to their gender and sexual identities. For students like Mark, the construction of their own family, varying by race, gender, and other identities, takes on heightened importance in their life, particularly for those who age out of the foster care system and face increased risks of homelessness and incarceration. For Mark, who is now a graduate student, his chosen family was developed, in part, through involvement in an LGBTQ+ alliance and the Latinx cultural center on campus—spaces where he felt he could be himself fully:

> Before I went to college, I didn't really feel like I could be myself. I had struggled with my identity for so long; it was refreshing to finally be in a place where I could just be. The people I met on campus [through the student organizations and campus] became my family. They will be at my wedding and godparents of my kid, if I have any. I don't have that kind of relationship with my [biological family].

The sense of belonging to a family for students with intersecting marginalized identities, whether those be race, gender, sexual orientation, or foster care history, takes on heightened importance as they are more vulnerable to isolation. Chosen family, thus, can act as a buffer, countering disconfirming messages students might be exposed to and subsequently internalize about themselves and their place and fit in the world, and certainly at an academic institution. As one student, Jordan, described it, it is through the unconditional love and support from her chosen family that she has navigated her college journey: "It's just having someone in your corner the way you would expect your [biological] family to be there for you but aren't. I'm grateful for them . . . and I got their back the way they got mine."

Students shared stories about the ways in which their chosen family stepped in to provide support for them, including Dylan, who relied on his family for support during the pandemic to meet his basic needs, or NiQi, who talked about spending holidays like Christmas and Thanksgiving with her chosen family. In NiQi's case, the formation of her family was organized around a shared experience of strained or nonexisting relationships with biological family.

The notion of chosen family can operate as a significant protective factor, enabling the persistence and success of students in college. The experiences of students in this study underscore broader recognition of these non-traditional, but very real, support systems that can be foundational to their well-being.

Self-Advocacy and Agency to Navigate College

Access to college and even navigation beyond the initial transition requires, dare I say demands, a certain degree of self-advocacy and agency, traits that many students with foster care experience have often honed through their life experiences. This section delves into how their capacity to effectively do so, shaped by their experiences in the foster care system, operate as a protective factor in their college-going journey, thus enabling their persistence and success.

Many of these students, having navigated through foster care, are quite adept at speaking up for themselves and challenging decisions or policies that don't align with their best interests. This propensity to do extends to and beyond their college experience. Consider this story from Mia, who recalled a time when her financial aid almost jeopardized her enrollment:

> I learned early on to be my own advocate and just [how] to speak up for myself. I remember one time [the school] messed up my financial aid. I forgot what exactly happen[ed], but they were saying I owed when I didn't. So, I had to meet like three different people, and eventually the dean of students because they weren't helping me. If I didn't do that I wouldn't be in school right now.

Mia's experience highlights not only her skillful navigation of bureaucratic hurdles but also the skepticism and diminished confidence in systems that she and so many other students with foster care background report. As a result, they often seek out support and resources rather than waiting for systems to serve them, as Mia described:

> I just think people aren't always inclined to help you, so I help myself and make sure I'm good. I don't ever just accept an outcome, well I mean sometimes you have to, but I always ask questions and I will always double check. For instance, I was able to get some scholarship money simply by asking someone in the financial aid office if they had money for students in foster care.

This theme of self-advocacy also resonates with a story from Isabelle, a science major who regretted missing out on an academic enrichment program and resolved never to let such opportunities slip through her fingers again:

> I always think back to that experience. It makes me take advantage of as much stuff as I can now that I'm in college. I'm always figuring on how to make things happen and advocate for myself and others like me.

These stories from Mia and Isabelle illustrate how some youth harness their experiences in the foster care system to adopt a proactive stance toward resources and supports needed for their success in college. Indeed, the capacity for self-advocacy and agency not only facilitates the transition to college but also acts as an asset and protective factor throughout their academic journey. Numerous students discussed their strategies for leveraging campus resources, from proactively researching scholarships to utilizing mental health services, and the importance of questioning campus staff and faculty for information and resources. Their adept use of campus support services, as revealed in the demographic questionnaire they completed prior to the interview, signifies a widespread recognition among these students of the value of self-advocacy in navigating their college journey.

In essence, these stories illuminate the importance and power of self-advocacy and agency as potentially transformative tools for students with foster care experience. Indeed, they can enable these students to navigate and overcome the challenges of higher education. Through their own words, we gain insight into how they transform their past adversities into assets.

Financial Literacy and Independence

Basic needs insecurity is a considerable challenge that is all too common for youth in care, and it can compromise their ability to persist in college. However, development of financial literacy and ultimately independence can act as a protective factor.

That some youth with foster care experience enter college with a heightened awareness of financial management and a desire for independence is not surprising, as it is often a result of necessity. Such awareness can be an important skill, however, enabling some students to navigate the host of financial decisions that shape their college experiences—from decoding financial aid packages to day-to-day budgeting and planning. For one student, Carlos, it was part of the reason why he was motivated to become an accounting major. "I didn't come from a family that was good with money . . . and when you're in foster care, you're worried about so many things but especially money. I just didn't want to be in that position again," he shared.

Concerns about meeting basic needs emerged as a prominent theme among most students in the study, especially those who aged out of care. However, some turned this concern into action, resulting in their investment in their financial savvy as they strove for independence. Wendy shared her desire to maintain a job on top of her academic studies despite not necessarily needing it:

> I've been working since I was sixteen . . . and I still work now [on campus]. All my expenses are covered for the most part, but I save as much as possible . . . you know, just in case something happens. I've learned to be pretty good with money, and I don't want to ever go without.

The heightened vigilance that Wendy experiences, fearing that she might again face financial instability, creates a sense of urgency to save and develop healthy money management habits. As a result, she can focus on her studies without worrying about the impact of a potential disruption in her finances. This desire for financial independence and stability also makes some students frequently search out additional financial supports and resources on and off campus, whether it be scholarships, grants, or other programs with financial incentives. Taylor generated a method of staying on top of it all:

> I created this spreadsheet, and I track all the different things I might qualify for each year and try to remember to apply to all of them. For me, it's [about knowing] that I'm going to be good no matter what happens.

This sense of independence that comes with financial security can be empowering for students. It's not just about making it through college with little debt, as one student noted:

> It's about taking control of my life and making sure that I have a good foundation for my future. We don't learn enough about being independent when you're in foster care . . . everybody is making decisions for you and then all sudden you are on your own and have to figure it out. Most kids have parents to help them figure it out. We don't have a plan B . . . well let me speak for myself. I don't have a plan B.

For Carlos, it was not enough for him to be financially savvy alone. He talked about wanting to help others through his campus support program for youth with foster care backgrounds, especially given his background in accounting. Indeed, he helped to lead financial literacy workshops for others and committed to helping his peers achieve the same independence and peace of mind that he enjoys. These workshops were geared not toward budgeting but to helping his peers to develop more healthy financial decisions overall, such as developing good credit, and investments—things that they might otherwise not be exposed to until much later in life.

Financial literacy and independence are more than just practical skills for students with foster care backgrounds; they are vital components of a protective framework that supports their academic persistence and success. Through the stories of students like Carlos, we see the transformative power of financial education—not just to survive the present but as a foundation for their future.

CONCLUSION

The purpose of this chapter was to offer insight into some of the salient protective factors for young people in foster care navigating college-going and pursuing their goal of degree completion. Dylan's story of resilience during the pandemic, enabled by a constellation of individual and environmental protective factors, coupled with the broader themes explored around racial and foster care identity development and empowerment, chosen families, self-advocacy and agency, and the importance of financial literacy and independence, together, paint a more robust picture of just some of the "bridges" to success for these students.

The agency and resilience demonstrated by these students are awe-inspiring, for sure. Yet they also reflect an unfortunate reality of systemic shortcomings. It is the responsibility of systems to operate in ways that serve and best meet the needs of the most vulnerable, such that students aren't required to be resilient or gritty. The stories from students shared in this chapter underscore the importance of proactive and student-centered approaches to policy and practice on campus to create environments where all students, regardless of whether they possess family privilege, can thrive.

As I will address more in depth in the next and last chapter, it is our responsibility to ensure that the bridges to postsecondary retention, persistence, and success are accessible to all students, paving the way for a future where every student can reach their full potential.

CHAPTER 6

Conclusion

Throughout this book, I have taken care not just in telling the precious stories of the young people my team and I learned from, but to highlight the nuanced experiences that punctuate their journeys. My aim was not to dwell on the doom and gloom, despite the serious challenges these young people confront and navigate. Instead, I focused on illustrating their agency, resistance, and resilience in the face of systemic challenges and shortcomings. Now, as I bring this book to a close, I invite you to pause and reflect—not just on the power of their stories, but on what their stories reveal about our responsibility to construct a world, and education and foster care systems, that effectively meet the needs and improve the material lives of one of our most vulnerable groups.

From my personal journey and near entry into the foster care system to the stories of students who navigated it, I have uncovered some of the ways in which the foster care system too often falls short of its mission. One of the ways it does this is through chronic residential instability—the constant shuffling and uprooting of youth from placement to placement, with such instability being more frequent and pronounced for those with marginalized identities. Issues of safety and security within the system were also troubling. That some youths are uprooted out of their homes due to concerns with safety and security, only to be placed in unsafe and unfit environments, is a deep system failure. And we saw, through Ma'Khia's tragic story, what is unfortunately possible when this happens. Counterproductive relationships with caseworkers emerged as a salient finding. Indeed, those charged with zealously advocating and supporting vulnerable young people seem to sometimes do the opposite—serving as sources of frustration and disappointment rather than encouragement and nourishment.

Against this backdrop of challenges, however, youth resist. They harness and transform negative experiences to assert their agency and independence. They learn how to skillfully maneuver and navigate systems and structures that otherwise conspire in their silencing and marginalization. We saw this in the story of Missy, a young Black girl, who, despite the lack of support from her caseworker, she leveraged her guardian ad litem to advocate for herself—a role that no young person should have to play to ensure they are supported in ways they are legally entitled to.

We also saw the power of "a hope in the unseen"—how some young people leverage their past experiences to formulate goal-directed thoughts, identify pathways for their educational goals, and become motivated to accomplish such goals. Hope, though a positive psychological phenomenon, emerges as a powerful lever for young people in care, explaining at least in part how some not only maintain high hopes for themselves but accomplish such aspirations. To be sure, that some youth require hope to persist in and through inequitable systems is a problem in and of itself and requires attention.

For youth of color, we see the power of community cultural wealth—those undervalued (by society) forms of capital that are inherent to people of color, which they activate to navigate systems that aren't designed for them and certainly don't serve them well. The constellation of these factors coalesces in ways that enable one to chart a path toward their dreams of college. We saw this in Barbie's remarkable story—specifically, the ways that aspirational capital inherent in her family's values about education and her navigational skills in maneuvering through the education system played a role in her education path.

From navigating the intersecting challenges of bullying and stigma to issues of school mobility and the lack of supportive adults to provide advocacy, we see youth demonstrate remarkable resilience. The notion of resilience should not be overglorified, as it comes with consequences for students. I wish for the day when an enormous amount of resilience is not needed for young people to experience life and pursue their dreams.

I also turned readers' attention to the complex process of accessing college—specifically, how some young people choose colleges born out of their fundamental desire to belong—to identify and secure places that align and are supportive of their identities. Places where they feel safe to be. In that chapter, I presented new and compelling insights into how some youth navigate the predisposition, search, and selection phases of college choice in ways that illustrate their motivation to satisfy their desire to belong.

Finally, I turned our attention to the bridges, not barriers, that enable persistence and success beyond the transition to college. Through student narratives, we heard firsthand how they navigated a global pandemic that produced challenges with basic needs insecurity and the important role of the ability to define one's own family. We explored how foster and racial identities coalesce in shaping their empowerment and the importance of financial independence and security.

Yet, the insights gleaned from these stories point to a larger reality: the success of these students is not solely a testament to their resilience. Rather, it also underscores a significant gap in the support provided by our education and child welfare systems—a gap that necessitates immediate and comprehensive action. As such, this conclusion is not an end but a beginning—a call to action for policymakers, educators, administrators, and all stakeholders in the student ecosystem to take deliberate steps toward dismantling the barriers that hinder the success of youth from foster care backgrounds. In the following section, I highlight some areas that should certainly be prioritized.

1. ENSURE PLACEMENT STABILITY AND DECREASE SCHOOL MOBILITY WITH ATTENTION TO EQUITY

The issue of placement stability in foster care, as demonstrated through the stories of students in this study, is of paramount concern. Multiple changes in placement are not only traumatic but also have consequences for school mobility, thus creating educational disruptions that hinder the academic progress and stability of young people. When youth experience abrupt and frequent moves between residential placements, this often results in multiple school changes, disrupting their social ties and relationships, making it difficult for them to adjust to school and perform well academically. This issue is compounded for students with minoritized identities, who often face additional layers of discrimination and bias in their placement experiences. Better coordination between child welfare agencies and educational institutions is necessary to address this challenge with an equity-minded approach.

The most recent authorization of the Every Student Succeeds Act (ESSA) in 2015 includes provisions that require every child to remain in their school of origin, unless it is determined not to be in their best interest. Moreover, educational institutions must collaborate with child welfare agencies to ensure the coordination of transportation and support for the young person. However, we know virtually nothing about the fidelity of implementation of these provisions—that is, what is happening on the ground to carry this out as intended. Such insights are key.

In addition to better system coordination, it is important to involve youth and their voices in decisions that concern them, like their placement and education. This includes actively involving students in conversations about their needs and preferences, with particular attention to the experiences of students of color and LGBTQ+ youth. Their voices are crucial in this process, helping to identify the best options as articulated by and for them.

2. EXTEND FOSTER CARE NATIONALLY

Basic needs insecurity among youth aging out of foster care is a critical challenge that compromises students' ability to succeed academically. It is time for federal policymakers to act, extending foster care services up to age 26. Such an approach would standardize support across the United States, ensuring that all young people, regardless of their state of residence, receive the necessary assistance they very much need as they transition into adulthood. Currently, the decision to extend foster care beyond the age of 18 lies with individual states, leading to a patchwork of policies that can result in unequal access to support for young people.

By implementing a national policy, we can eliminate this inconsistency and provide a stable foundation for these young adults, mirroring the support often provided by families to their children during their transition into higher education and early career paths. Such a change would align with standard practices in health care as it relates to allowing young adults stay on their parent's insurance plans until age 26. A uniform approach to extending foster care would demonstrate a national commitment to the well-being and success of all young people, ensuring that they have the support needed to thrive.

3. PREPARE K–12 EDUCATORS TO SUPPORT YOUTH IN FOSTER CARE

Teacher education programs nationwide must integrate training focused on young people in foster care, using an intersectional lens. Unlike other underserved student populations, such as those who are racially/ethnically minoritized, low-income, LGBTQ+, or homeless, youth in foster care—who intersect with all these identities disproportionately—are often overlooked in teacher education program curricula and training. This neglect adds to the precarity of this population and fuels the marginalizing experiences they encounter within their school contexts. Training should cover fundamental awareness of how trauma affects their lives, issues related to school disruptions, and the bullying and stigma they may face, enabling teachers to foster supportive classroom environments for them.

Additionally, future educators need to be equipped to advocate effectively for youth in care, not only within schools but also in partnership with child welfare services. Teachers occupy a crucial role in the lives of young people in care, a responsibility that should be recognized with specialized preparation to address the unique challenges these students encounter.

4. STATES SHOULD APPOINT OMBUDS OFFICERS FOR CHILDREN AND FAMILIES

Every state should establish a dedicated Ombuds Office to support youth and families. Such an office could serve several important roles, including but not limited to addressing challenges and issues that parents experience within the system and providing a resource for youth who have concerns and grievances. It would investigate and seek to resolve complaints made by or on behalf of these young individuals, like the complaints shared in this study. Drawing on models like the one implemented in Ohio after the tragic loss of Ma'Khia Bryant, this Ombuds Office should be granted access to child welfare records and data from both public and private foster care agencies. This access is vital for conducting thorough investigations and advocating effectively for systemic improvements.

Like the model in Ohio, these offices should be mandated to produce annual reports that document findings, challenges, and suggestions for reforms within the system. Following the example in Ohio, leadership for this office might be appointed by the governor. This would help ensure a high level of accountability within the state. To ensure that youth voices are prioritized as well, states should leverage youth advisory boards, if they don't already.

Offices like this could provide much-needed aid for youth and families who don't feel well supported by existing structures, while their creation would also be an important signal from the state about its commitment to the welfare of its most vulnerable. Establishing this office is just one step forward toward a more transparent, responsive, and just child welfare system.

5. IMPLEMENT EARLY COLLEGE AWARENESS AND PREPARATION PROGRAMS

Local and state leaders should invest in the development and evaluation of early college awareness and preparation programs tailored to young people in foster care. Like programs designed for other underrepresented groups, these initiatives would aim to introduce these young individuals to the opportunities available in higher education from an early stage. By offering comprehensive support services such as tutoring, college tours, and guidance through the application process, these programs can significantly demystify the path to college.

Starting such programs early is critical, ensuring that young people with foster care experience can see higher education as a realistic and achievable goal. This proactive approach helps cultivate a college-going mindset, effectively countering disconfirming messages one might receive about their place and fit in education. Tailoring these programs to the unique challenges and needs of young individuals with foster care experience not only makes the dream of higher education more attainable but also demonstrates a commitment to equity and support for all students, irrespective of their backgrounds.

6. PROVIDE YEAR-ROUND CAMPUS HOUSING

To effectively support students transitioning from foster care, addressing their basic needs, particularly housing insecurity, is crucial. San Francisco State University (SFSU) has emerged as a leading example in this effort by becoming the first public university in the country to offer year-round housing to students from foster care backgrounds. By dedicating up to 40 spots in the Towers at Centennial Square Apartments specifically for these students, without incurring additional costs to the university, SFSU addresses a critical gap in support during academic breaks, when many of these students face potential homelessness (Blackshear, 2013).

This initiative is part of the broader Guardian Scholars program at SFSU, which offers a range of supports, including academic, social, financial, and emotional assistance, to former youth in care. The provision of stable housing throughout the year is a key component of this program, significantly contributing to the students' academic success and overall well-being.

SFSU's approach not only addresses the immediate housing needs of former youth in care but also sets a precedent for how universities can utilize existing resources to support this vulnerable student population. This model demonstrates the importance of an institutional commitment to fostering an inclusive and supportive academic environment for all students, particularly those who have experienced the foster care system. Other colleges and universities are encouraged to consider similar initiatives, ensuring that students from foster care backgrounds receive the support they need to succeed academically and personally.

7. INVEST IN CAMPUS SUPPORT PROGRAMS FOR YOUTH IN FOSTER CARE

There has already been a surge in the development of campus support programs designed to address the needs of youth in foster care. One example is the previously mentioned Guardian Scholars Program in California, which is a multi-campus program that plays an important role in providing comprehensive support services that cater to the unique needs of these students. The challenge with such programs, however, is that there is very little uniformity in how they are implemented. Ideally, they should take their cues from proven strategies that effectively address the challenges these youths face. Coupled with adequate financial backing, standardization can enhance the impact of these programs across various institutions.

It is also important for program staff to be adequately prepared to support young people with marginalized identities. Indeed, such programs must be designed and carried out in ways that acknowledge, respect, and affirm, students' diverse experiences and identities, ensuring that services are not inadvertently centered around a "White-normed" perspective. By doing so, support programs can become more inclusive and effective in meeting the nuanced needs of all students, particularly those from underrepresented and marginalized communities.

8. ADDRESS FAMILY PRIVILEGE AND EDUCATIONAL TRADITIONS

Recognizing family privilege and how traditional family structures are often prioritized in education is vital. Students coming from conventional family backgrounds generally find educational environments more tailored to their experiences, inadvertently placing youth in foster care at a disadvantage. It's essential to broaden our understanding of family to include "chosen family"—the supportive networks that individuals form outside of biological ties, which are especially crucial for youth with foster care experience.

For example, events like Parents' Weekend at colleges can unintentionally highlight these disparities. Such traditions, while meant to foster community and inclusion, can instead feel isolating for students without traditional family support. A more inclusive approach could involve reimagining these events to celebrate a wider array of supportive relationships, such as "Family and Supporters' Weekend," explicitly welcoming chosen family members, mentors, and significant individuals who play a pivotal role in students' lives.

Educational institutions must acknowledge the diverse family structures that students come from while also validating the importance of non-traditional support systems. By making room for broader conceptions of family and adapting traditions to be more inclusive, schools and colleges can create environments where all students, regardless of their family background, feel valued and supported.

FINAL THOUGHTS

The recommendations provided here are just a starting point, not an exhaustive list. Accepting institutional responsibility for young people in foster care involves acknowledging their experiences and dedicating ourselves to addressing the systemic barriers that hinder their educational and life success. We must collectively work toward transforming higher education into a space that is equitable and supportive for every student, especially those affected by the foster care system. It's our shared responsibility to build bridges to higher education that don't rely solely on the resilience of these students but that are undergirded by strong, equitable and accessible support systems designed to meet their specific needs. This effort requires the creation of inclusive policies that tackle the root causes of their struggles, the enhancement of support programs for comprehensive and ongoing assistance, and the cultivation of campus environments where every student is made to feel valued, understood, and capable of reaching their highest potential.

An Overview of the Study

From Foster Care to College originated from a narrative inquiry project my research team and I launched in 2019, before the onset of the COVID-19 pandemic, and that we continued through 2021. Narrative inquiry is a method that examines human experiences through storytelling (Clandin & Connelly, 2004; Lieblich et al., 1998). I selected this approach to underscore the often-muted voices and experiences of youth impacted by foster care. This method was not about "giving voice" to these individuals, as they inherently possess their own powerful voices. Rather, my aim was to collaborate with them to *amplify* their powerful stories.

Recognizing that knowledge is socially constructed, we (the interpreters) collaborated with students (the interpreted) to construct meaning from their experiences. This approach aligns with a constructivist framework (Crotty, 1998), and I also aimed to be critical in this work. This involved not only collaborating with students to narrate their stories but also critiquing and challenging the oppressive structures that have shaped their experiences (Abes & Wallace, 2018; Kincheloe, 2008).

The design of this study was enriched by the input of a Community Advisory Board (Savage et al., 2021) that included four individuals: two graduate students with direct experience in foster care, a student affairs practitioner who directs a college support program for such students, and a local community activist who was previously in foster care. Their insights were useful in conceptualizing the study, reviewing interview protocols, assisting in participant recruitment, deciphering insider terms and concepts related to foster care, and providing feedback on interpretations of findings. They played a vital role in ensuring the authenticity and sensitivity of our approach, and I am deeply grateful for their thought partnership in sharpening the study's focus.

STUDENT RECRUITMENT

Most qualitative studies on college youth with foster care experience typically focus on relatively small samples limited to a specific context, such as a program, set of programs, or institutions within a particular region (Johnson, 2021). To be sure, such approaches are valid and characteristic of qualitative research. However, I sought to broaden our recruitment efforts to a more national scale. This decision was driven by the need to assemble a sufficiently diverse sample across race, institution type, gender, and sexual orientation.

In contrast to previous research that predominantly centered on students at 4-year institutions (Johnson, 2021), we extended this study to encompass students attending 2-year community colleges as well. The only requirement was that participants had spent some time in foster care. Consequently, we did not restrict participation solely to students who had aged out of the foster care system, a focal point of many previous studies (Johnson, 2021).

To purposefully recruit participants, we devised a recruitment email and flyer that were approved by the institutional review board (IRB) in charge of monitoring research ethics at our university, which we shared via email to program coordinators and directors of campus-based support programs for students with foster care backgrounds. We collected their contact information from publicly available sources online. Additionally, we leveraged the connections of our Community Advisory Board (CAB), whose involvement proved invaluable in our recruitment efforts.

We also used social media platforms, such as X (formerly "Twitter"), Facebook, and Instagram, to share our recruitment flyer. This online outreach significantly helped us in reaching potential participants who appreciated our commitment to this crucial work. Furthermore, we actively engaged student organizations, community programs, and advocacy groups that focused on youth in foster care.

To expand our sample's diversity, we also used snowball sampling techniques. Participating students were encouraged to share information about the study with their peers who met our study criteria. After the initial wave of data collection, we implemented maximum variation sampling to further diversify our sample. For example, it was imperative for a significant portion of our sample to include Black students, as they are disproportionately affected by the foster care system but are often underrepresented in both quantitative and qualitative research samples (Johnson, 2021). Additionally, we made it a priority to ensure representation of LGBTQ+ students. Our collective efforts yielded a diverse sample of 49 students who participated in interviews.

DATA COLLECTION

While I am appreciative of the efforts of college and university IRBs across the country who ensure that social science researchers like me carry out their work in ethical ways that also shield study participants from harm, especially those from vulnerable groups, I don't always find their requirements sufficient. As the principal investigator (PI) of this study, it was important to me that my team and I were prepared to engage with participants in ways that firmly recognized their humanity.

I trained members of my research team who assisted in data collection in trauma-informed approaches to interviewing. This training equipped them with the knowledge and skills necessary to create a safe and supportive environment for participants. To ensure their well-being, I developed "care protocols." These protocols were specifically designed to help our team navigate questions that were potentially triggering for students, providing them with guidance on how to approach those moments with sensitivity and empathy.

Our primary goal was to prioritize the emotional and psychological well-being of the students over the research itself. Period. These protocols underscored the importance of informed consent; flexibility in interview scheduling; and the use of nonintrusive, open-ended questions. We also emphasized the need for ongoing support, referrals to mental health professionals, and debriefing sessions after each interview, if necessary. Our commitment to trauma-informed interviewing was integral to the ethical and respectful conduct of our research.

Ok, now, in terms of data collection, this involved two steps. All participants were invited to complete an online survey designed to gather essential demographic details, such as race/ethnicity, gender, sexual orientation, and age. This survey also delved into their academic profiles, capturing information about their year in school, major field of study, GPA, and journey through the foster care system, including duration and residential placements.

Subsequently, we extended an invitation to the students to complete two to three comprehensive life story interviews. These interviews were structured around the framework established by McAdams's Life Story Interview format (McAdams, 2013) and supplemented by the Ecological Systems Interview Tool (Kitchen et al., 2019). This approach was geared toward uncovering significant events, characters, and themes that defined each student's personal narrative, paying close attention to their various ecological contexts over time, such as their experiences in foster care, K–12 education, community or neighborhood influences, and their journey in postsecondary education.

The first of these interviews aimed to elicit detailed narratives about the participants' identity perception and recounting of past experiences that shaped their lives. We explored various spheres of their lives, from their foster care stories to their educational journeys and community influences. In the follow-up interview, we sought to clarify and delve deeper into these narratives, focusing on the intricacies of their experiences and their transition into college life. We also encouraged participants to share their aspirations and their strategies for achieving them, with questions like "What are your earliest memories of your thoughts about college?" and "Think back to when you were first accepted for college. What did you do to prepare?" A $30 Amazon gift card was provided as a token of appreciation after the completion of the second interview.

The onset of the COVID-19 pandemic in the spring of 2020 introduced an unforeseen dimension to our study. Recognizing the unique challenges posed by the pandemic, especially for students impacted by foster care, we conducted follow-up interviews with those who were currently students. These conversations centered around their experiences during the pandemic, probing their sense of community connectedness and coping strategies in these unprecedented times. We were careful to steer these discussions away from a purely deficit-based narrative, instead focusing on resilience and adaptability. Participants in these additional interviews also received a $30 Amazon gift card and a document that my team created with tailored resources to aid young people in foster care during the pandemic. Each interview typically lasted between 45 to 75 minutes. We conducted a total of 120 interviews.

DATA ANALYSIS

The data collected in this project were extensive, encompassing 2,000 pages of interview transcripts and reflective memos. To ensure accuracy, my team and I meticulously reviewed these transcripts, cross-referencing them with the audio recordings to correct any inaudible or unclear sections. For data management and coding, I utilized ATLAS.ti, a sophisticated computer-assisted qualitative data analysis software. This tool was instrumental in organizing and categorizing the vast amount of data.

The analytical approach was two-pronged, focusing on both the unique content of each participant's story and the common themes emerging across narratives. I employed Lieblich et al.'s (1998) categorical-content method for narrative data analysis, which began with a thorough review of the transcripts to immerse myself in the data. During this process, inductive codes were identified based on emerging patterns. My team supported this effort by conducting independent reviews, ensuring a comprehensive analysis.

Simultaneously, I developed deductive codes derived from my conceptual frameworks. These codes were instrumental in guiding the analysis toward relevant themes and concepts inherent in the data. The amalgamation of inductive and deductive codes led to the creation of a comprehensive codebook, as recommended by McQueen et al. (1998). This codebook served as the foundation for the systematic analysis of the narratives, uncovering the intricate layers of each participant's experiences in foster care and its role in their educational journey.

THE STUDENTS

The study includes 49 diverse students who brought a wide range of experiences and important dimensions of social identity into focus. Here is some crucial demographic and background information about them:

- *Ethnicity and Race:* The students exhibited diversity in terms of their ethnic and racial backgrounds. The breakdown included 16 White students, 15 Black students, 9 Hispanic/Latinx students, 5 multiracial students, and 4 Asian/Pacific Islander students.
- *Gender:* Most of the students identified as cisgender women (33), while 14 were cisgender men, 1 identified as nonbinary, and 1 as a trans woman.
- *Sexual Orientation:* Most of the students identified as heterosexual (30). Nine students identified as bisexual, 3 as gay, 3 as pansexual, 3 as lesbian, and 1 as queer.
- *Age:* The students' ages spanned a wide range, indicating a diverse group that included adult learners. The youngest student was 18 years old, while the oldest was 41.
- *Enrollment Status:* Almost all the students were currently enrolled in higher education, with 2 being graduate students. Those not enrolled were recent college graduates.
- *Undergraduate Institution:* Most students in the sample attended 4-year colleges and universities (88%), with the remaining 12% attending 2-year community colleges.
- *Year in School:* Among the surveyed students, 20.41% were in their freshman/1st year, 26.53% were sophomores/2nd year, 18.37% were junior/3rd-year students, 20.41% were seniors/5 or more years into their college journey, and 4.08% were graduate students.
- *Major:* The academic majors among the 49 students were diverse. The most prevalent major was social work, with

18.37% of students majoring in it. Other prominent categories included social sciences (16.33%), natural sciences (16.33%), and fine arts and human services and health-related majors (both at 12.24%). Additionally, 8.16% majored in business and finance, 4.08% in communication and media or computer science and technology, and another 4.08% in legal studies and criminal justice. A smaller portion, 2.04%, studied mathematics and philosophy, showcasing the variety of academic disciplines represented among the students.

- *High School GPA (HS GPA) and College GPA:* Our analysis of the students' academic performance revealed a range of GPAs. The median high school GPA was 3.4, while the median college GPA was 3.0. Additionally, the average high school GPA was 3.24, and the average college GPA was 3.12. These figures provide insight into the academic achievements of our participants and their transition to higher education.
- *Foster Care Experience:* The data on time spent in foster care and residential placement changes revealed a wide range of experiences among the individuals in the study. The duration in foster care varies from as short as 1 year to over 20 years, with a substantial portion having spent 9 to 10 years in care. Residential placement changes also vary significantly, with some individuals having experienced as few as one placement change and others enduring over 100 changes, according to their accounts. Moreover, 51% "aged-out" of foster care. These numbers underscore the diversity and complexity of the students' journeys through the foster care system.
- *School Placement Changes:* The data on school placement changes among the students indicated a wide range of experiences. Some students reported having changed schools frequently, with numbers exceeding 10 changes in some cases. Conversely, a few students mentioned having experienced no school changes at all. The variability in school placement changes emphasizes the challenges and disruptions these students may face in their education.
- *Incarceration History:* Out of the students in the sample, approximately 28% had experienced periods of incarceration, while the remaining 72% did not have any involvement with incarceration.

It's important to note that the demographic data mentioned above were all self-reported by the students.

References

Administration for Children and Families. (n.d.). Foster care. U.S. Department of Health & Human Services. https://www.acf.hhs.gov/cb/focus-areas/foster-care

Alexander, M. (2010). *The new Jim Crow: Mass incarceration in the age of colorblindness*. The New Press.

An, E. M., Lee, S. J., & Chung, I. J. (2020). The effects of the stigma trajectory of adolescents in out-of-home care on self-esteem and antisocial behavior. *Children and Youth Services Review*, *116*, 105167.

The Annie E. Casey Foundation. (n.d.). What is foster care? https://www.aecf.org/blog/what-is-foster-care

Antle, B. F., Johnson, L., Barbee, A., & Sullivan, D. (2009). Fostering interdependent versus independent living in youth aging out of care through healthy relationships. *Families in Society: The Journal of Contemporary Social Services*, *90*(3), 309–315. doi:10.1606/1044-3894.3890

Augsberger, A., & Swenson, E. (2015). "My worker was there when it really mattered": Foster care youths' perceptions and experiences of their relationships with child welfare workers. *Families in Society*, *96*(4), 234–240.

Berger, M. T. (2010). *Workable sisterhood: The political journey of stigmatized women with HIV/AIDS*. Princeton University Press.

Billingsley, A., & Giovannoni, J. M. (1972). *Children of the storm: Black children and American child welfare*. Harcourt Brace Jovanivich.

Blackshear, R. (2013, October 16). Campus provides year-round housing for foster youths. *The Imprint: Youth and Family News*. https://imprintnews.org/news-2/campus-provides-free-year-round-housing-for-students-of-foster-care-system/4181#0

Brooms, D. R., & Clark, J. S. (2020). Black misandry and the killing of Black boys and men. *Sociological Focus*, *53*(2), 125–140.

Child Welfare Information Gateway. (2022). *Extension of foster care beyond age 18*. U.S. Department of Health and Human Services, Administration for Children and Families, Children's Bureau. https://www.childwelfare. gov/topics/systemwide/laws-policies/ statutes/extensionfc/

Clandinin, D. J., & Connelly, F. M. (2004). *Narrative inquiry: Experience and story in qualitative research*. John Wiley & Sons.

Clemens, E. V., Klopfenstein, K., Tis, M., & Lalonde, T. L. (2017). Educational stability policy and the interplay between child welfare placements and school moves. *Children and Youth Services Review*, *83*, 209–217.

Conley, D. T. (2007). Redefining college readiness. *Educational Policy Improvement Center (NJ1).*

Courtney, M. E., Okpych, N. J., & Park, S. (2018). Report from CalYOUTH: Findings on the relationship between extended foster care and youth's outcomes at age 21. Chapin Hall Center for Children at the University of Chicago.

Courtney, M. E., Terao, S., & Bost, N. (2004). Midwest evaluation of the adult functioning of former foster youth: Conditions of youth preparing to leave state care. Chapin Hall Center for Children at the University of Chicago.

Crotty, M. J. (1998). *The foundations of social research: Meaning and perspective in the research process.* Thousand Oaks, CA: Sage.

Destin, M., & Williams, J. L. (2020). The connection between student identities and outcomes related to academic persistence. *Annual Review of Developmental Psychology*, 2, 437–460.

Dettlaff, A. J., & Boyd, R. (2020). Racial disproportionality and disparities in the child welfare system: Why do they exist, and what can be done to address them? *The ANNALS of the American Academy of Political and Social Science*, *692*(1), 253–274.

Dworsky, A., & Pérez, A. (2010). Helping former foster youth graduate from college through campus support programs. *Children and Youth Services Review*, *32*(2), 255–263.

Fergus, S., & Zimmerman, M. A. (2005). Adolescent resilience: A framework for understanding healthy development in the face of risk. *Annual Review Public Health*, *26*, 399–419.

Foster, E. M., Hillemeier, M. M., & Bai, Y. (2011). Explaining the disparity in placement instability among African-American and White children in child welfare: A Blinder–Oaxaca decomposition. *Children and Youth Services Review*, *33*(1), 118–125.

Fostering Connections to Success and Increasing Adoptions Act of 2008. (2008). Public Law No. 110–351, § 101, 122 Stat. 3949.

Geiger, J. M., & Beltran, S. J. (2017). Readiness, access, preparation, and support for foster care alumni in higher education: A review of the literature. *Journal of Public Child Welfare*, *11*(4–5), 487–515.

Gizir, C. A., & Aydin, G. (2009). Protective factors contributing to the academic resilience of students living in poverty in Turkey. *Professional School Counseling*, *13*(1), 2156759X0901300103.

Gleeson, J. P., Wesley, J. M., Ellis, R., Seryak, C., Talley, G. W., & Robinson, J. (2009). Becoming involved in raising a relative's child: Reasons, caregiver motivations and pathways to informal kinship care. *Child & Family Social Work*, *14*(3), 300–310.

Goffman, E. (2009). *Stigma: Notes on the management of spoiled identity.* Simon and Schuster.

Gross, J. P. (2019). *Former foster youth in postsecondary education: Reaching higher*. Springer.

Gross, J. P., & Geiger, J. (2019). An overview: Foster care and policies designed to support youth in care. In J. P. Gross (Ed.), *Former foster youth in postsecondary education: Reaching higher* (pp. 39–59). Palgrave MacMillan.

Harris, M. S. (2021). Racial bias as an explanatory factor for racial disproportionality and disparities in child welfare. In A. J. Dettlaff (Ed.), *Racial disproportionality and disparities in the child welfare system* (pp. 141–158). Champ, Switzerland: Springer.

Hass, M., Allen, Q., & Amoah, M. (2014). Turning points and resilience of academically successful foster youth. *Children and Youth Services Review, 44*(9), 387–392.

Hass, M., & Graydon, K. (2009). Sources of resiliency among successful foster youth. *Children and Youth Services Review, 31*(4), 457–463.

Hausmann, L. R., Schofield, J. W., & Woods, R. L. (2007). Sense of belonging as a predictor of intentions to persist among African American and White first-year college students. *Research in Higher Education, 48*, 803–839.

Hossler, D. and Gallagher, K. (1987) Studying college choice: A three-phase model and the implications for policy makers, *College and University*, Vol. 62, pp. 207–221.

Hull, K. E., & Ortyl, T. A. (2019). Conventional and cutting-edge: Definitions of family in LGBT communities. *Sexuality Research and Social Policy, 16*, 31–43.

Iloh, C. (2019). An alternative to college "choice" models and frameworks: The Iloh model of college-going decisions and trajectories. *College and University, 94*(4), 2–9.

Jalongo, M. R. (2006). The story of Mary Ellen Wilson: Tracing the origins of child protection in America. *Early Childhood Education Journal, 34*, 1–4.

James, S. (2004). Why do foster care placements disrupt? An investigation of reasons for placement change in foster care. *Social Service Review, 78*(4), 601–627.

Johnson, R. M. (2013). Black and male on campus: An autoethnographic account. *Journal of African American Males in Education (JAAME), 4*(2), 103–123.

Johnson, R. M. (2021). The state of research on undergraduate youth formerly in foster care: A systematic review of the literature. *Journal of Diversity in Higher Education, 14*(1), 147.

Johnson, R. M. (2021). *Black youth in foster care and the school–prison nexus. Feature: The community college context* (Vol. 6, no. 3). Office of Community College Research and Leadership.

Johnson, R. M. (2021, May 6). Foster care awareness: Ma'Khia Bryant's death calls attention to the system's deep-rooted issues. *Essence*. https://www.essence.com/news/foster-care-awareness-makhia-bryant/

Johnson, R. M. (2022). A socio-ecological perspective on sense of belonging among racially/ethnically minoritized college students: Implications for equity-minded practice and policy. *New Directions for Higher Education*, 2022(197), 59–68.

Johnson, R. M., & Dizon, J. P. M. (2021). Toward a conceptualization of the college-prison nexus. *Peabody Journal of Education, 96*(5), 508–526.

Johnson, R. M., Strayhorn, T. L., & Parler, B. (2020). "I just want to be a regular kid": A qualitative study of sense of belonging among high school youth in foster care. *Children and Youth Services Review, 111*, 104832. https://doi.org/10.1016/j.childyouth.2020.104832

KIDS COUNT Data Center. (2020). Black children continue to be disproportionately represented in foster care. https://datacenter.kidscount.org

Kincheloe, J. L. (2008). *Critical pedagogy primer* (Vol. 1). Peter Lang.

Kirk, C. M., Lewis, R. K., Nilsen, C., & Colvin, D. Q. (2013). Foster care and college: The educational aspirations and expectations of youth in the foster care system. *Youth & Society*, *45*(3), 307–323. https://doi.org/10.1177/0044118X12451025

Kitchen, J. A., Hallett, R. E., Perez, R. J., & Rivera, G. J. (2019). Advancing the use of ecological systems theory in college student research: The ecological systems interview tool. *Journal of College Student Development*, *60*(4), 381–400.

Konijn, C., Admiraal, S., Baart, J., Van Rooij, F., Stams, G. J., Colonnesi, C., Lindauer, R. & Assink, M. (2019). Foster care placement instability: A meta-analytic review. *Children and Youth Services Review*, *96*, 483–499.

Latalova, K., Kamaradova, D., & Prasko, J. (2014). Perspectives on perceived stigma and self-stigma in adult male patients with depression. *Neuropsychiatric Disease and Treatment*, 1399–1405.

Lieblich, A., Tuval-Mashiach, R., & Zilber, T. (1998). *Narrative research: Reading, analysis, and interpretation* (Vol. 47). Sage.

MacQueen, K. M., McLellan, E., Kay, K., & Milstein, B. (1998). Codebook development for team-based qualitative analysis. *Cam Journal*, *10*(2), 31–36.

Maslow, A. H. (1943). Preface to motivation theory. *Psychosomatic medicine*, *5*(1), 85–92.

Masten, A. S. (2001). Ordinary magic: Resilience processes in development. *American Psychologist*, *56*(3), 227.

McAdams, D. P. (2008). *The life story interview*. Northwestern University. http://www.personality-arp.org/html/newsletter06/teaching_interview.doc

Myers, J. E. (2008). A short history of child protection in America. *Family Law Quarterly*, *42*(3), 449–463.

National CASA. (2009). National CASA association aims to eliminate the foster care stigma [Press release]. http://nc.casaforchildren.org/files/public/site/PressReleases/Feb2009_Study_Release.pdf

Neal, D. (2017). Academic resilience and caring adults: The experiences of former foster youth. *Children and Youth Services Review*, *79*, 242–248.

Noguera, P. A. (2003). Schools, prisons, and social implications of punishment: Rethinking disciplinary practices. *Theory into Practice*, *42*(4), 341–350.

Okpych, N. J. (2021). *Climbing a broken ladder: Contributors of college success for youth in foster care*. Rutgers University Press.

Okpych, N. J. (2022). Estimating a national college enrollment rate for youth with foster care histories using the National Youth in Transition Database (NYTD): Limitations of NYTD and a call to revise and relaunch. *Journal of Public Child Welfare*, *18*(1)1–26. https://doi.org/10.1080/15548732.2021.2010635

Okpych, N. J., Courtney, M. E., & Charles, P. (2015). *Youth and caseworker perspectives on older adolescents in California foster care: Youths' education status and services*. Chapin Hall at the University of Chicago. https://www.chapinhall.org/research/study-of-foster-youths-education-status-finds-many-are-facing-hurdles-to-success/

Okpych, N. J., & Park, S., Courtney, M. E., & Powers, J. (2021). *Memo from CalYOUTH: An early look at predictors of college degree completion at age 23 for foster youth*. Chicago, IL: Chapin Hall at the University of Chicago.

Papovich, C. (2020). Trauma & children in foster care: A comprehensive overview. *Forensic Scholars Today*, *5*(4), 1–5.

Pecora, P. J., Kessler, R. C., O'Brien, K., Roller White, C., Williams, J., Hiripi, E., English, D., White, J., & Herrick, M. A. (2006). Educational and employment outcomes of adults formerly placed in foster care: Results from the Northwest Foster Care Alumni Study. *Children & Youth Services Review*, *28*(12), 1459–1481. https://doi.org/10.1016/j.childyouth.2006.04.005

Pelton, L. H. (2010). Introduction: Race, class, and the child welfare system. *Journal of Health and Human Services Administration*, 270–276.

Perna, L. W. (2006). Studying college access and choice: A proposed conceptual model. In *Higher education: Handbook of theory and research* (pp. 99–157). Dordrecht: Springer Netherlands.

Riebschleger, J., Day, A., & Damashek, A. (2015). Foster care youth share stories of trauma before, during, and after placement: Youth voices for building trauma-informed systems of care. *Journal of Aggression, Maltreatment & Trauma*, *24*(4), 339–360.

Roberts, D. (2009). *Shattered bonds: The color of child welfare*. Hachette UK.

Rose, A. L., Atkey, S. K., Flett, G. L., & Goldberg, J. O. (2019). Self-stigma and domains of well-being in high school youth: Associations with self-efficacy, self-esteem, and self-criticism. *Psychology in the Schools*, *56*(8), 1344–1354

Rubin, D. M., O'Reilly, A. L., Luan, X., & Localio, A. R. (2007). The impact of placement stability on behavioral well-being for children in foster care. *Pediatrics*, *119*(2), 336–344.

Rutter, M. (1996). Transitions and turning points in developmental psychopathology: As applied to the age span between childhood and mid-adulthood. *International Journal of Behavioral Development*, *19*(3), 603–626.

Sanchez, R., Morales, M., & Carroll, J. (2021, April 22). Ma'Khia Bryant argued about housekeeping before fatal police shooting, foster parent says. *CNN*. https://www.cnn.com/2021/04/22/us/ohio-columbus-makhia-bryant-police-shooting/index.html

Savage, S. S., Johnson, R. M., Kenney, A. J., & Haynes, D. D. (2021, October). Perspectives on humanizing and liberatory qualitative research with racially/ethnically minoritized youth. *Healthcare*, *9*(10), 1317. MDPI.

Scherr, T. G. (2007). Educational experiences of children in foster care: Meta-analyses of special education, retention and discipline rates. *School Psychology International*, *28*(4), 419–436. https://doi.org/10.1177/0143034307084133

Seita, J. R. (2018). History of foster care: Policy, practice, and reformation. In E. Trejos-Castillo & N. Trevino-Schafer (Eds). *Handbook of foster youth* (pp. 3–19). Routledge.

Sewell, W. H., & Shah, V. P. (1968). Parents' education and children's educational aspirations and achievements. *American Sociological Review*, *33*(2), 191–209.

Smith, J. M. (2017). "I'm not gonna be another statistic": The imagined futures of former foster youth. *American Journal of Cultural Sociology*, *5*, 154–180.

Stanton-Salazar, R. (1997). A social capital framework for understanding the socialization of racial minority children and youths. *Harvard Educational Review*, *67*(1), 1–41.

Strayhorn, T. L. (2018). *College students' sense of belonging: A key to educational success for all students*. Routledge.

Suskind, R. (2010). *A hope in the unseen: An American odyssey from the inner city to the Ivy League*. Crown.

Tobolowsky, B. F., Scannapieco, M., Aguiniga, D. M., & Madden, E. E. (2019). Former foster youth experiences with higher education: Opportunities and challenges. *Children and Youth Services Review*, *104*, 104362.

Trammell, R. S. (2009). Orphan train myths and legal reality. *The Modern American*, *5*(3).

Tuck, E. (2009). Suspending damage: A letter to communities. *Harvard Educational Review*, *79*(3), 409–428.

U.S. Department of Health and Human Services. (2021). *Adoption and foster care analysis and reporting system*. Administration for Children & Families. https://www.acf.hhs.gov/cb/report/trends-foster-care-adoption

Whitman, K. L. (2016). Students on the margins-margins: A critical examination of research on African American foster youth in higher education. *Urban Education Research & Policy Annuals*, *4*(1), 47–54.

Yosso, T. J. (2005). Whose culture has capital? A critical race theory discussion of community cultural wealth. *Race Ethnicity and Education, 8*(1), 69–91.

Index

About the Author

Royel M. Johnson is a nationally recognized scholar, speaker, and consultant. He is Associate Professor of Higher Education and Social Work at the University of Southern California (USC), where he also serves as PhD chair in the Rossier School of Education. He is also the director of the National Assessment of Collegiate Campus Climates in the USC Race and Equity Center—the nation's leading tool for assessing campus racial climate. An expert and consultant on college access, student success, and organizational change for racial equity, Johnson has published over 60 peer-reviewed articles, chapters, and reports. His work appears in respected outlets such as the *Journal of Higher Education*, *Teachers College Record*, and *Education Administration Quarterly*. He has coedited four books: *Racial Equity on College Campuses: Connecting Research and Practice* (SUNY Press), *Enacting Student Success: Critical and Alternative Perspectives for Practice* (Jossey Bass), *Creating New Possibilities for the Future of HBCUs with Research* (Information Age), and *The Big Lie About Race in America's Schools* (Harvard Education Press). Dr. Johnson's work has been funded by organizations such as the U.S. Department of Education, Spencer Foundation, and Chan Zuckerberg Foundation, totaling more than $6.3 million. He is also coeditor of *Educational Researcher*, the flagship journal for the American Education Research Association (AERA). For his exemplary scholarly contributions, he was awarded the 2022 Early Career Award from AERA Division G, along with several other early career honors from AERA, ACPA-College Educators International, and both of his alma maters, the University of Illinois at Urbana Champaign and Ohio State University.